THE POWER OF CURIOSITY

"I own two businesses and have always felt like an ineffective boss. I knew my product was successful, but I had trouble delegating and motivating my staff. After reading *The Power of Curiosity*, my relationships with my staff have completely changed. I no longer dread having to have meetings with my employees, instead I am excited to hear their thoughts and learn from them. My business has only become stronger, and my work environment is more creative and dynamic. My team is now passionate about their work—and the only thing I modified was approaching each situation with curiosity. Using the tools *The Power of Curiosity* has taught me, not only helps me be a better boss, it helps me be a better person. My husband, family and friends all feel more heard, seen and understood. By using the tools in this book, you open yourself up to learning more about your co-workers, your loved ones and yourself. A true gift."

Sue Bell, Founder of Giggles and
Grass Stains Creative Learning Center

"Kathy Taberner and Kirsten Siggins' work on being present when we listen to others, and choosing how to listen, has had a profound impact on my conflict resolution work as a mediator and negotiation trainer. *The Power of Curiosity* is a must read for learning how to apply these skills to our difficult conversations, and indeed all our conversations—to listen better, truly understand and connect with others, and move forward in our relationships—whether negotiating a large business contract, acting as leaders in our organizations, or enriching our personal relationships."

Colleen Cattell, ENS International Negotiation Consultant

THE **POWER** OF
CURIOSITY

How to Have Real Conversations
That Create Collaboration,
Innovation and Understanding

KATHY TABERNER AND
KIRSTEN TABERNER SIGGINS

NEW YORK

THE POWER OF CURIOSITY

How to Have Real Conversations That Create Collaboration, Innovation and Understanding

© 2015 KATHY TABERNER AND KIRSTEN TABERNER SIGGINS.

Published in New York, New York, by Morgan James Publishing. Morgan James and The Entrepreneurial Publisher are trademarks of Morgan James, LLC.
www.MorganJamesPublishing.com

The Morgan James Speakers Group can bring authors to your live event. For more information or to book an event visit The Morgan James Speakers Group at www.TheMorganJamesSpeakersGroup.com.

A **free** eBook edition is available
with the purchase of this print book.

CLEARLY PRINT YOUR NAME ABOVE IN UPPER CASE

Instructions to claim your free eBook edition:
1. Download the BitLit app for Android or iOS
2. Write your name in **UPPER CASE** on the line
3. Use the BitLit app to submit a photo
4. Download your eBook to any device

ISBN 978-1-63047-394-5 paperback
ISBN 978-1-63047-395-2 eBook
ISBN 978-1-63047-396-9 hardcover
Library of Congress Control Number:
2014948518

Cover Design by:
Rachel Lopez
www.r2cdesign.com

Interior Design by:
Bonnie Bushman
bonnie@caboodlegraphics.com

In an effort to support local communities, raise awareness and funds, Morgan James Publishing donates a percentage of all book sales for the life of each book to Habitat for Humanity Peninsula and Greater Williamsburg.

Get involved today, visit
www.MorganJamesBuilds.com

Habitat
for Humanity®
Peninsula and
Greater Williamsburg
Building Partner

*To all our clients who have shared
their wisdom about the importance of
curiosity, and to our family for their
patience and support.*

CONTENTS

FOREWORD

I feel extremely privileged to write this foreword to *The Power of Curiosity*. The book you hold in your hands rightfully belongs in the leadership section, the parenting section, the self-help section, the healthcare section, and the "change the world" section of any bookstore. But most importantly, it belongs on your tablet, or your personal shelf of "the good books," so you can reference it often.

Perhaps like many of you, my earliest recollection of the concept of curiosity came from reading the Curious George books (particularly *Curious George Goes to the Hospital*, which may have been the book that ignited my passion for healthcare as a career). Thinking back on Curious George now, I see how he used the power of curiosity to access that innate, insatiable desire to learn more, spark the passion for discovery, be present in the moment, and take risks.

The Power of Curiosity gives us access to all of this and more. As Kathy and Kirsten show us, we are all born with curiosity, but as adults this natural gift is forgotten or dampened down for a variety of reasons.

I hadn't realized that I, too, was a victim of this all-too-common loss of curiosity until I started my master's degree in leadership, where I met Kathy, and soon thereafter, Kirsten.

As the Director of Learning and Development at a large tertiary healthcare facility in British Columbia, I partnered with Kathy when our organization engaged her to facilitate an aspect of a healthcare leadership development program and provide coaching to front-line leaders. I had always loved learning and growing, particularly in my career as a registered nurse, healthcare leader, and executive coach. But I hadn't realized that the key to my next level of growth was developing my self-awareness—by becoming curious about myself.

Since then, I have known Kathy as my colleague, coach, mentor, fellow learner, and friend. I always enjoy our conversations, which are authentic, thought provoking, and inclusive—and usually involve a glass of wine! Kathy's eyes twinkle and her face lights up when she discovers yet another context in which she can live out the state of curiosity.

In the same way, I love how Kirsten has taken a coaching approach to parenting. The stories she shares of her kids demonstrate a parenting style that is respectful and models the skills of deep listening and genuine inquiry. She is a wonderful role model for her children and has set the stage for the beginnings of the "relational generation."

I am in awe of their special bond as mother and daughter, which is also evident throughout the book. They are a synergistic duo, and I have personally witnessed their practice of curiosity individually, with each other, with colleagues, with their families, and with clients.

Kathy and Kirsten have given us the gift of this book to aid in our adoption of this new practice of curiosity. The more we can embrace this practice, the more it can become a way of being in the world and unleashing our power to take risks, challenge the status quo, deeply listen, and intently learn. In Part One, Kathy and Kirsten help us "relearn" the Curiosity Skills that used to come so naturally as children. (The ABSORB acronym is my new daily mantra that I have on my bulletin board in my office and on my iPad screen.) In Part Two, they help us apply our newly rediscovered Curiosity Skills through understanding ourselves: knowing our values, setting boundaries, naming and noticing emotions, and taming those emotions—setting the stage for understanding others. They summarize this process brilliantly in Part Three, presenting a step-by-step way to manage ourselves in relationship with others and answer what they call the "million-dollar question": How can we engage in authentic, respectful dialogue, even amidst tension? Accessing the power of curiosity opens the gate to *be* in relationship with others and move through conflict while keeping those relationships intact.

My own mantra—"it's all about the learning"—is strengthened and validated through this book. Curiosity paves the way for true learning: learning about self and learning about others so that we can learn together in relationship. I offer my best wishes, utmost gratitude, and appreciation to Kathy and Kirsten for a fine piece of work that will help shape new ways of thinking, new ways of behaving, and new ways of relating for so many.

With gratitude,
Dori Van Stolk
Director, Learning & Development
BC Children's Hospital and BC Women's Hospital + Health Centre
Founder, ensoGroup Coaching and Consulting, Inc.
August 2014

INTRODUCTION

THE MILLION-DOLLAR QUESTION

I (Kirsten) am sitting in a doctor's office with my five-year-old son, tense and ready for a fight. This is our third ear, nose, and throat specialist (ENT) in two years, and I have been assured this one is "the best." My son has been having 106-degree fevers for virtually all his life. Every individual fever had been attributed to a very reasonable cause: an ear infection, a virus, a cold. But no one could explain why he kept getting these high fevers over and over again. After countless tests, medical experts had assured us that there was nothing "scary" wrong with him—therefore, he was "fine." Yet deep in my bones I knew something wasn't right. My friends kept telling me not to be the "crazy parent," and eventually I learned to keep my worries to myself.

That is, until today. After my son's eardrum erupted the previous night, and I was once again sitting in bed with my five-year-old in uncontrollable amounts of pain, I vowed I wouldn't accept the "he is fine" verdict anymore.

As we wait for the ENT, I find myself screaming in my head, "Why will no one listen to the whole story?!" This time, I don't care if the doctor thinks I am crazy. I will say and do whatever it takes to get my son the help he needs.

We have all been here at some point in our life. Whether it's been at the doctor's office, at home, or at a staff meeting, someone tells us something that just doesn't seem right, and not wanting to cause a stir or seem ignorant, we simply accept what he or she has said. Yet because we don't fully understand, we remain frustrated beneath the surface. We may even feel helpless and vulnerable, as if we have no control over an outcome we are at least partially responsible to produce. The truth is that when we don't fully understand someone or a situation, it leads to conflict, whether external or internal. At that point, it doesn't take long for our emotional buttons to get pushed, and we find ourselves either saying things we regret or withdrawing and retreating in silence, saying nothing about the frustration that continues to simmer beneath the surface.

I was desperate to understand what was happening with my son and felt trapped because I couldn't have the conversations I needed without getting emotional or feeling like I was crazy. In my head, I wanted clear, rational discussions about how to move forward and get full understanding; however, in my heart, I was insanely frustrated and was willing to say and do anything at any cost.

So how do we have an authentic exchange of thoughts and feelings, one that promotes respectful, productive dialogue and leads us to a place of calmness, confidence, and abundance—even in high-stakes situations?

As a mother/daughter executive coaching team, this has been the million-dollar question at the core of both our personal and professional lives, as the way we communicate in emotionally charged scenarios tends to be the same whether we're at home or at work. It's true for us, and it's certainly true for our clients. Over the last ten years we have been working with leaders interested in achieving new and different outcomes with their teams—outcomes that build collaboration, innovation, and stronger relationships. However, when our clients wanted more from their teams, they often got emotional. They found themselves getting stuck in a judgmental headspace, where they were right and their team members were wrong. Not surprisingly, they resorted to telling others what to do and how to do it.

Although these leaders thought their decisiveness was communicating competence, they were, in fact, messaging that their teams were incompetent and couldn't figure out how to do it "right" themselves. When the teams wouldn't engage or the results were not achieved, these leaders would blame, judge, criticize, and even shame. But this leadership style was not producing the results they wanted either, leaving our clients frustrated and stuck in behavioral ruts they didn't know how to get out of.

Why is this important? It is important because we are in the middle of a paradigm shift. We are shifting from the more hierarchal Industrial Era to a more collaborative Information Age. Our advances in technology may now be considered the single greatest influence in our lifetime. They have made dreams once considered inconceivable come true: we have flown to the moon and made a home in space; we can see the person to whom we're speaking even when she's in another hemisphere; we can transmit and receive information in less than a blink of an eye; we can support a cause, consult a doctor, offer an opinion, raise funds for a personal project, sell goods and services, download music, upload videos, and share our entire lives with the world from the comfort of our own home. We hold the world in our hands and see it unfolding in "real-time," overwhelming detail. Much of what we can imagine we have the means to achieve.

For the first time ever, we have a younger generation that has access to more information than the one before it. Older generations can no longer presume to know the experiences of those much younger than themselves. Effective leadership now requires a flatter, more transparent, collaborative approach, because the traditional top-down model of leadership no longer works—in the workplace or in the home. Just as an over-fifty employer can't begin to understand (or at the very least has trouble comprehending) the perspective of employees in their twenties, a parent of a seven-year-old can't comprehend the viewpoint of their child. Their world is an alien landscape in comparison to the parent's when she was seven or the manager's when she was in her twenties. With a computer in hand, a child or young employee can be as knowledgeable in any subject, or more so, than their parent or leader. The traditional knowledge-bearers must now adjust, at least in the area of technology, to sharing this role with their much-younger counterparts, and this can be a difficult adaptation—one to which most adults are unaccustomed.

In the Information Age, organizations want engagement, collaboration, innovation, inspiration, and accountability—skills that are currently expected of leaders yet aren't being taught. Even as the culture is swiftly changing, most people are not. For example, as parents, we still use our own parents as role models when we tell our children what to do. (Almost all parents have heard their own parents' words coming out of their mouths!) As leaders, we emulate the leadership styles we have experienced, resorting to a directive, controlling style when we feel our survival is at stake. As a professional, we may model our rapport with clients or patients on the approach of our mentors and others from whom we learned. That's why, when we experience negative emotions in certain situations, we automatically return to the hierarchical model and find ourselves saying things that later we wish we could retract.

Our clients knew very well that they needed to engage their teams and have conversations that allowed for an authentic exchange of thoughts and feelings and promoted a respectful, productive dialogue that supported learning. The problem was that they didn't know how to do it, and they were beginning to recognize that their go-to communication style was influenced by how their parents and teachers spoke to them when they were young.

In short, what our clients really needed and craved were *tools*, not theory. Specific, accessible tools that they could use anytime, anywhere that would support them in these emotional moments and help them identify opportunities in situations of potential conflict and achieve different outcomes. Wanting the same for ourselves, we set out to create those tools. With the help of our clients, we learned that relationships are *everything*—both professionally and personally. We learned that what we do is not as important as how we do it. We learned that a new language was needed to support leaders at all levels. And we learned that rarely, if ever, do we practice or develop the skills that are so fundamental to success in our relationships.

Since both of us are also mothers, we naturally began by thinking more about how our communication skills develop as young children. As toddlers, we are naturally curious, connecting with others in our world as we explore and learn how to have our needs met. As children, we are encouraged to collaborate, to learn and share with our friends and family. Yet beginning with our elementary school years, things begin to change. Our learning process becomes more isolated, as we share what we learn privately with our instructors through taking exams, writing papers, and solving problems as individuals, often discouraged to share answers, concepts, and ideas. Then, as teenagers, we begin to feel that we are constantly told what to do by the adults who have charge over us. It is an impressionable time to discover, learn, and emerge as young leaders, but it is also a time when adults tend to present themselves as knowing everything, thus implying the teenagers know nothing and (often unintentionally) judging, shaming, or blaming teens for the choices they make.

Then, it occurred to us: How can we become fully developed, highly effective adult leaders when we, at our most impressionable, are consistently told what to do by our parents, teachers, sports coaches, and other adults in authority? These adults, filled with good intentions, want to protect us so we don't stumble and fall or perhaps make the same mistakes they made—mistakes which are, in actuality, critical to learning. We are never taught how to listen, ask questions, or be curious about understanding ourselves and others; we are told to "do" these things with the assumption that we know how to do all of them well. Spoiler alert: we don't!

We are rarely taught how to identify our values, set boundaries, or determine what sends us into an emotional tailspin and why. Yet all three of these skills directly impact our success at work, at home, and in our relationships. For most of us, our early experiences shape our go-to language, one that is telling, judging, blaming, and even shaming—a language that influences our leadership and/or parenting style and how we build our relationships throughout our lives.

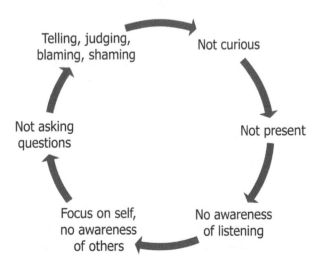

We will be honest: this journey was not one we intentionally set out to have. As we practiced and played with our ideas, what became abundantly clear was the *power of curiosity*. When we aren't curious, we don't listen. When we aren't curious, we are unable to have an open-minded point of view. When we aren't curious, we don't bother asking questions. When we aren't curious, we tell, judge, criticize, blame, and shame.

Quite simply, the skills we need to succeed are the Curiosity Skills we are born with but rarely nurture into adulthood: being present to actively listen, being aware of our listening choices in every situation, and asking curious, open questions to understand others' perspectives and points of view.

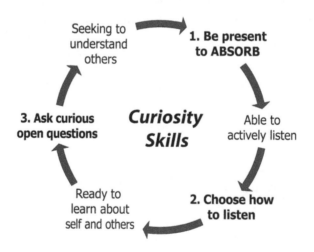

It really did seem that simple: the key to success was *curiosity*. So we began developing specific communication tools fueled by the power of curiosity and teaching them to our clients.

Interestingly, as we taught these communication skills within a workplace context, we noticed that our clients wanted to try them in the comfort of their own home first before using them in the workplace.

Then something happened that no one expected. Through practicing just three skills, the personal lives of our clients changed in very tangible ways. For example:

A nurse and mother of a twelve-year-old had been constantly frustrated with her son, as he rarely completed the chores she asked him to do. Wanting different results, she decided to take a more curious approach when discussing the chores with him, intentionally asking questions to understand what was keeping him from finishing his chores and actively listening to his perspective. With their new joint understanding, her son committed to completing his chores in a way that worked for him, rather than the way she would complete them. The son thanked his mom for helping them have a different conversation, one in which he felt she had actually listened to what he said. And the mother was thrilled that the chores were finally being completed!

An executive who was in an arranged marriage began playing with her Curiosity Skills at home and discovered that curious, open questions and active listening allowed her to find joy in her relationship. She was finally able to begin to understand and connect to her husband of several years.

A manager and grandmother of a young granddaughter used curiosity to help her figure out what was making her five-year-old granddaughter sad. Rather than assuming she knew the answer already, and telling her granddaughter what she needed and what would make her happy, the grandmother chose to listen and ask curious, open questions to understand her granddaughter. Together, they were able to solve the situation in a way that inspired the granddaughter to thank her grandmother for "being different," and that she liked it.

Once these executives saw the power of curiosity transform their most personal relationships, they began to apply what they learned at work. Rather than getting frustrated and telling their teams what to do, they became curious and asked their team members how they thought they should move forward, boosting morale and producing results they would have never have thought of. Rather than suffering in silence and constantly taking on more than they wanted to, they became curious about what they needed, set boundaries, and achieved different, better results. When clients got emotional and started to lose their cool, rather than slipping into the assumption of "I am right and you are wrong," starting heated arguments, or retreating in silence, they became curious and chose to listen, ask questions, and take the time to understand the other. This new approach consistently led to new opportunities they wouldn't have otherwise imagined.

Specifically, here is the dynamic we discovered. Without applying the Curiosity Skills:

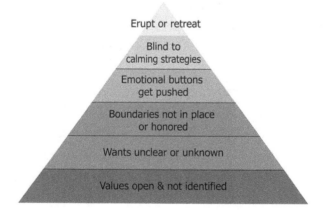

Applying the Curiosity Skills, on the other hand, creates new possibilities and opportunities and strengthens relationships.

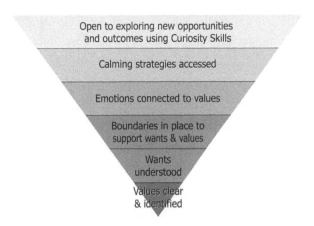

As with any change you make in your life, becoming curious will have a ripple effect throughout all areas of your life. You will see in this book that we will often alternate back and forth between personal and professional contexts, as the skills we are teaching are not just for work or just for home. These skills are a lifestyle. The more you practice and incorporate curiosity into all aspects of your life, the greater success you will have.

The method we will share with you has three parts. "Part One: The Curiosity Skills" will identify the three specific skills you need to incorporate into every aspect of your life in order to achieve the transformative outcomes you want: being present to ABSORB[1] what the speaker is saying, choosing how to listen in conversation, and asking curious open questions to understand. These three skills are going to help you shift from telling, judging, blaming, and shaming to being open to learning about yourself and others, which is exactly where new possibilities and opportunities become achievable.

In "Part Two: Using Curiosity to Understand Yourself," you will then apply the three Curiosity Skills to yourself, as understanding yourself is a crucial first step to understanding others. Here you'll

---

1   ABSORB is an acronym you'll learn more about chapter 2.

learn where conflict typically begins: at the level of our values. As our workplaces, homes, and communities become more diverse, conflicting values are inevitable—but our negative reactions to conflict are not! The solution to conflict is not to avoid it, but to recognize it and respond with curiosity to defuse negative emotions early on. Through the power of curiosity, you'll identify your values and your wants, implement appropriate boundaries, discover your own emotional triggers, and learn strategies to support yourself in those moments of potential conflict when you want to retreat or explode.

Finally, in "Part Three: Using Curiosity to Understand Others," we will put it all together. Now that you've learned the Curiosity Skills and have used them to better understand yourself, you can apply these skills to all of your conversations with others, even the most challenging. You'll learn a step-by-step process you can use in any conversation to avoid the discomfort of stress and fractured relationships altogether and transform potential conflict into positive outcomes and new opportunities.

Let's return to the ENT's office. Armed and ready, I (Kirsten) recount to yet another doctor the last five years of my son's life in painful, factual detail. Much to my surprise, he agrees: my son is not fine, and his health history does not make any sense. He looks me in the eye very calmly and says, "I am going to treat him like he is one of my own, and we are going to keep asking questions until we get the answers we need." I immediately disarm and want to cry. Although I haven't received any answers from this ENT, and we are no closer to understanding what is wrong with my son, for the first time I feel like I am being heard. He tells me we need another perspective, and he suggests we start with his colleague, the best immunologist and allergist in the city.

When I left his office that day, I felt empowered. We were working together as a team to uncover what was happening to my son, and as long as we stayed curious and kept asking questions, I knew we were going to get the answers we needed. We set up an appointment with the

ENT's colleague, and an allergy test solved our mystery—my son was allergic to over seventy of the substances he was tested for. The moment we changed his diet and removed the allergens, he was fine. Now he rarely gets sick, and he hasn't had a 106-degree fever since.

As the saying goes, "There is no greater distance between two people than misunderstanding." Understanding others is the sweet spot in life where we learn, connect, inspire, innovate, and collaborate. Our relationships are strengthened, our self-confidence is boosted, and anything becomes possible.

We all hold the power of understanding, and it begins with curiosity. Mahatma Gandhi asked us to be the change we want to see in the world. We *can* change the world, by our own example, one curious conversation at a time. We just need a method to remind us of what we already know. This book offers that method.

Part One

THE CURIOSITY SKILLS

CHAPTER 1

WHY CURIOSITY?

I have no special talents. I am only passionately curious.
Albert Einstein

A s kids, we are all curious. Kids are constantly asking questions, wanting to solve problems, looking for new possibilities. All because they are curious, wanting to learn more. Curiosity is a childhood survival skill; it's how they learn, test their assumptions, become open to new perspectives, push the boundaries of what they are capable of, make mistakes, *and* do things they (and often we) never thought were possible. As kids, time is a limitless commodity, and the present is the only place to be.

But somewhere along the way, as we grow into adulthood, we lose our sense of curiosity. Is it when our parents become frustrated with our millions of questions—as they're thinking about other things in their lives and are not present in the moment—and tell us to stop asking them or make us feel bad for asking them? Is it when our teachers, who don't have the time or means to answer the myriad of questions thrown at them, dismiss these questions or make us feel we aren't smart enough because we don't already know the answer?

Sadly, however it happens, curiosity in adulthood is hard to find. We live in a time-pressured world, always anticipating what is coming next with little time to be curious about what is happening now.

A recent *Globe and Mail* (BC) interview with Brigid Schulte, author of *Overwhelmed: Work, Love, and Play: When No One Has the Time,* pointed out that North Americans feel they are time constrained, which impacts their ability to be curious. [1] Our offices are now our homes; our homes are now our offices. Technology tracks our every move, "connecting" us with friends on social media. Expectations of people are high, and people are trying to do everything at once. As a consequence, our communication is brief and our instructions shallow, leaving little room for listening, inquiry, and understanding.

But curiosity shouldn't be something we grow out of. In fact, curiosity has been recognized as one of the most important skills needed by a leader today. In 2011, *Forbes* recognized curiosity as "the one trait all innovative leaders share," using the success of Steve Jobs as an example: "Jobs wasn't curious because he wanted to be successful. He became successful because he was so curious."[2]

What Is Curiosity?

Curiosity is one of the great secrets of happiness.
Bryant H. McGill

What does curiosity mean, and why is it so important? We think of curiosity as exploration: being inquisitive, seeking to learn and understand. Some associate curiosity with being nosy. After all, aren't we being nosy if we are curious about another person, asking personal questions? We believe there is a difference between the two. Nosy people ask questions and proceed to judge the answers provided. Their intention is not to learn about the other person, but to compare, perhaps wanting to determine who is better or worse. In contrast, true curiosity holds no judgment. It is about exploring and learning with the goal of greater understanding, which is free from judging. When curious people ask a question, their only intention is to better understand, whether it is another person, an idea, a place, an origin, or anything that creates an interest in further exploration.

We are, in fact, wired for curiosity as human beings. Findings in neuroscience have confirmed that when we are curious about something, the hormones dopamine and oxytocin, our natural "feel good" chemicals, are released in our brains. Not only do these hormones make us feel good, they also create a connection between the heart and the brain that leads to a greater sense of openness. As a result, we experience a greater sense of connection with others, which supports the creation of a new, shared reality based on understanding.[3]

A New Communication Paradigm

Of course, curiosity does more than make us feel good. As we mentioned in the Introduction, we believe it can help us successfully navigate our transition from the hierarchical Industrial Era to the more collaborative Information Age. Specifically, curiosity can form the basis of a new communication paradigm that helps us create the conversations we need to better understand other perspectives and view increased diversity as a positive opportunity rather than a challenge or a threat.

This new communication paradigm can help fuel innovation in any context, whether it's organizations wanting collaboration, innovation, inspiration, transparency, and engagement from their employees, or parents wanting to avoid making the same "mistakes" their parents made with them.

Before we get into the specific skills of curiosity this new communication paradigm includes, let's take a closer look at the specific communication shifts we need to make and how curiosity can fuel these shifts.

Old Communication Paradigm	New Communication Paradigm
Telling	Asking
Judging	Accepting
Blaming	Non-blaming
Excluding	Including
One perspective	Diverse perspectives

Shift from Telling to Asking

Based on our experience with our clients, telling is the most common approach to leadership, parenting, and conversing with others. People love to tell others what to do; they believe providing advice is "helpful," even if the advice is not requested. Telling worked in the Industrial Era because it was hierarchal in structure. This communication style implied the teller inherently had valuable information to provide and knew the correct solution, suggesting the recipient of the advice was less knowledgeable than the teller. In the Information Age, people have more equal access to knowledge and, with the help of technology, are generally able to find their own solutions. If someone wants advice, they will ask for it. In general, telling is no longer well received. It can be perceived as lacking in respect, narrowing opportunities and shutting down possibilities by implying that the individual is incapable of solving a problem.

When Telling Is Useful: There are times, however, where telling is important and needed. Professionals who have years of training are sought out for their knowledge and expertise. They are expected to tell, advise, or prescribe. It is why people hire them. However, transferring this approach to conversations with colleagues or family is less effective, once again implying (whether intentionally or not) they are better or wiser than the person being offered the advice.

As an occupational therapist and physician coach, I (Kathy) have worked a great deal in the healthcare industry and find healthcare professionals are effective tellers when diagnosing, prescribing for, and working with patients. Unfortunately, there is a tendency to use this same approach in meetings with colleagues. For example, some of my coaching clients with leadership roles in the healthcare industry notice, when chairing meetings, their teams tend to move very quickly through meeting agendas. The first one to speak offers a solution, and others tend to accept this solution and want to move on to the next item without discussion. At the same time, others don't say a word, even though these leaders know those individuals have great ideas and could contribute if given an opportunity.

How can leaders incorporate curiosity into such a situation? As they begin to use their Curiosity Skills, they shift from telling to asking open questions that encourage dialogue and the generation of ideas. As a result, their team is able to create better solutions—solutions their team will willingly buy into and be accountable for. Some leaders even create agendas where each item is stated as an open question, encouraging everyone to be curious about the issues at hand and contribute to the conversation.

Curiosity provides leaders an opportunity to approach conversations differently, as equal participants who want to better understand others, not just tell them what to do—directly meeting the needs of leadership today. Telling is such an important communication characteristic that we have devoted an entire chapter to it (chapter 4), where we will show you how to use the Curiosity Skill of asking open questions, giving you a deeper understanding of when to ask and when to tell.

Shifting from Judging to Accepting

"Don't judge me!" is an expression we hear so frequently these days. We find people in our society are becoming super aware of when they are being judged and are speaking out, often defiantly. So why do we judge?

For most people, judging is a coping mechanism used to ensure they see themselves as better than (or less than) others. It helps people differentiate themselves. Such situations can occur every day when the "gremlin" voice inside their heads is constantly criticizing others, deciding their way, their style, or their expression is better or worse than another's. It helps people feel superior or inferior, which for some is needed to thrive. We see it as a throwback to the Industrial Era when we all thought in hierarchal terms.

Let's use a practical example. Imagine you are a leader of a team, and a team member has submitted a report you feel is shockingly bad. It's incomplete, inaccurate, and you are embarrassed to have a team member submit such work to you. You know they can do better than this. You ask your team member to meet with you and the conversation goes something like this:

> **Leader**: "You have written a really bad report. In fact, it is incomplete, inaccurate, and just plain useless."
>
> **Team member**: "I am sorry. I thought I had written exactly what you told me to write."

Leader: "No, you obviously did not listen. This is full of mistakes and the format is all wrong. I can't believe you did such a sloppy job. Go and do it again. See if you can be smarter this time!"

As the leader, how are you feeling? How do you think this team member is feeling? How have you supported this team member to write a better report? Have you engaged your team member, or inspired them to improve? How productive do you think this team member will be moving forward?

Now, as the leader, imagine that rather than judging this team member's work, you chose to be curious about the reasons she completed it this way.

Leader: "I have just read your report, and I don't think it is up to par. What do you think of it?

Team member: "I am not sure what I think about it. Although I thought a different approach might be more effective, I decided I should use the one suggested at our last meeting."

Leader: "What source did you use to obtain the information you included?"

Team member: "I retrieved all the information from our files on the cloud."

Leader: "I am wondering—how accurate do you think the information is on our cloud?"

Team member: "I found the information to be outdated. I think I can contact the other managers and ask them to provide me with their current information, which will be more accurate."

Leader: "What format did you use?"

Team member: "The format used was the one agreed to at the last meeting. How would you like to see the report formatted?"

Leader: "I am not sure. I want the information to be easy to read and presented so I can easily look at both years and see what has changed."

Team member: "It sounds as if you want to be able to easily compare one year to another. I have a different format I have been playing with and can show you if you want. I think it provides the information in a more user-friendly way that better meets your needs."

Leader: "I would appreciate seeing the other format. I like the idea of going directly to the other managers. When do you think you can have a revised report on my desk?"

Team member: "I will send you a copy of my suggested format and circulate it to the other managers for their input, if you like. I should be able to get the information from each of them in the next three days and have the revised report on your desk by the end of the week, provided the format is agreed upon."

Leader: "Sounds good. I would appreciate you forwarding me your suggested format as soon as possible, and I agree the other managers should see it. Thanks."

As the leader, what did you notice? How do you think this team member is feeling now?

Looking at the two examples above, which example is most in line with your leadership style?

While the second conversation took slightly longer, it had a very different outcome. Each became curious about how they arrived at the place where the report produced did not meet their standards. Rather than judging the team member based on what the leader thought was right or wrong, this communication approach was open to new possibilities, accepted that there was more than one way to approach writing a report, and created the opportunity to co-create the desired outcome. In the long run, the second conversation is much more likely to produce a report that meets the needs of the leader, team, and organization.

When we judge others, we become closed to understanding them and therefore reject them based on their choices. In contrast, when we become curious, we choose to understand them, become open to new perspectives, find common ground upon which we can build agreement, and accept that there is not just one way to do anything.

When Judging Is Useful: Although judging is frequently criticized in our society, like so many other traits it can be valuable at the appropriate time and place. Judgment is fundamental for any expert as they make recommendations, develop ideas, and make needed decisions. Judgment is also valuable in the context of moral issues, ethics, safety issues, and emergencies. People look to the leader who has sound judgment and can make quick decisions in times of crisis. This kind of judgment is not what we are referring to in the examples above. In chapter 4, we will talk about how the Curiosity Skill of asking curious, open questions can shift unhelpful judgment to acceptance.

Shift Blaming to Non-blaming

How often do you walk away from a conversation feeling you have done something wrong—and you have no idea what you've done? How did you feel? How does it affect your relationship with the person casting blame on you? Blaming can make us feel inadequate, not good enough, hurt, upset, or ashamed. Sadly, feeling blamed can happen any time. Our society seems to be hardwired to find someone to blame for anything perceived to have gone wrong. Whether we are at the office, home, online, or offline, blaming is a universal language, and we often do it without realizing it.

We find it interesting that people jump to conclusions in so many situations, assuming a particular person is to blame for whatever has just occurred. We are all human, and as such are all very capable of making mistakes. Mistakes provide a great opportunity for one to learn; however, if blame is added to the mix, how does it impact the learning moment? What is the expectation when we blame someone? How do we know they have learned anything from the mistake that was made?

Imagine you are one of four office assistants at an organization. Part of your job is to keep the storeroom neat and organized, which involves moving heavy boxes, unpacking them, and organizing their contents so everyone can access items easily. Safety is very important to your organization; they have rules, everyone knows, that ensure no one lifts too much weight, so employees are expected to ask for help from another when moving the heavy boxes. You worked in the storeroom three days ago and pushed some of the boxes around. You took the next two days off complaining of back pain. When you returned to work, Ann, the office administrator, wanting to ensure safe practices, decides to have a conversation with you about this incident.

Ann: "Hi. I understand you hurt your back working in the storeroom three days ago."

You: "Yes, I was pushing boxes around that were full. I found I needed to lift one over another, and I strained my back."

Ann: "You know there is an expectation that you never lift a box by yourself. Why would you do this?"

You: "I thought I could do it by myself."

Ann: "You are a good employee, and I expect more of you. You know the rules about safety. Please make sure this never happens again."

You: "Yes, Ann."

As an office assistant, how are you feeling when you leave Ann's office? How are you feeling about having Ann as your supervisor?

What have you learned that will help you do things differently next time? How does Ann know that you, as the office assistant, will never do this again?

The reality is that nothing has changed, and no learning has occurred. You, the office assistant, likely feel blamed and through fear may never make the same mistake again; however, you may repeat the error because you have learned nothing. For one to change a behavior, one needs to learn how to do something differently to ensure the same thing doesn't happen again.

Rather than blaming you and expecting you to change, what if Ann, the office administrator, chose to get curious about what happened and how you were going to ensure it wouldn't happen again?

Ann: "Hi. I understand you were working in the storeroom three days ago, lifted a heavy box, and hurt your back. How is your back feeling now?"

You: "My back is feeling much better, thank you."

Ann: "Given we all know the rules about lifting boxes, and there is a notice in the storeroom that states them, what was your reason for attempting this?"

You: "Yes, I do know the rules and was not planning to lift the box. I thought I could just move it along the floor to where it needed to go. I had received a complaint from one of the managers that the boxes were not being unpacked in a timely way, and he asked me to take care of it right away. I knew no one else was available to help me, and I thought I could push it along the floor by myself."

Ann: "How come no one else was available to help you?"

You: "I decided I would start while everyone else was on their break, so there was no one available, and I wanted to get the work done so the manager would be happy. I also had a lot of other things to complete that day."

Ann: "How come you chose not to take your break when everyone else was on theirs?"

You: "I didn't think I needed a break and wanted to get the storeroom organized as quickly as possible, so I decided not to take my break. I had other things I needed to complete that day, and I thought I could get everything completed on time this way."

Ann: "How could you have approached this differently?"

You: "I could have done the photocopying that was needed later that day, and then when someone returned, asked for help moving the boxes. I just hate asking for help."

Ann: "I find you to be an employee who likes to get work done in a timely way and can appreciate your desire to get everything completed. I also know it is hard for any of us to ask for help. Our culture is all about employee safety. What can you do differently next time such a request is made, so you adhere to the rules we have created to ensure our safety?"

You: "I will try to keep the storeroom organized on an ongoing basis so there is no need to rush to organize it because someone finds it messy. I know there is plenty of time during the day when I can ask for help, and I will do so on a regular basis so we can keep the storeroom tidy. I will also try to prioritize my work so that I do the tasks I can do alone when there is no one available to help me. I think I also need to take my breaks so I don't feel stressed out and do too much."

Ann: "It sounds as if you have a plan. What do you need to help you keep to this plan?"

You: "I think I can do this. Having back pain was not fun. I know I need to ask for help, and I think I can do this."

Ann: "Good to talk to you, and I hope your back has fully recovered."

You: "Thanks, Ann. Good-bye."

At the end of this meeting, as the office assistant, how are you feeling and what have you learned? How do you think Ann is feeling? How are you feeling about Ann as your supervisor?

Looking at these two approaches, although the second one took slightly more time, it is still a short conversation. The second approach, rooted in curiosity, provided an opportunity to learn and to change behavior, leaving no room for blame. While it is easy to blame others, and may even make you feel better when you do, how does it help you as a leader (or parent) achieve the desired outcome? How does blame support learning, accountability, or building strong relationships?

When Blaming Is Useful: Granted, many societies use the approach of casting blame (resulting in punishment) to support the morals of the system. But outside this context, we do know that blame in and of itself serves little useful purpose, as learning is not supported, and without learning, changes in behavior are extremely difficult to achieve.

Take a moment and reflect on how often you find yourself blaming others. What new possibilities or opportunities could you create if you replaced blame with curiosity? In the next three chapters, we will give you the specific Curiosity Skills you can use to avoid blame and engage curiosity.

Shifting from Excluding to Including

While reflecting on the needs of organizations, leaders, and families today, we realized that one of the standout characteristics is inclusivity. Why? Because inclusivity supports what everyone ultimately wants from their relationships: collaboration. Yet the majority of leaders, organizations, and families are still using the language of the old paradigm in which one person—typically the oldest, most educated, and/or wealthiest—makes all the decisions, and their decisions rule with little discussion or inclusion of others, resulting in exclusivity. Today, this person could be a director, CEO, or other senior leader of an organization. There is no need for others to pipe in with ideas because they are considered inadequate or wrong. Yet research shows that exclusivity in problem solving, even with a genius, is not as effective as inclusivity, where everyone's ideas are heard and a solution is developed through collaboration.[4]

Exclusion is also seen in some families where parents (or maybe older children) feel no need to include other family members in decisions that involve most or all of them. Typically the parent is exclusive, feeling it is his or her responsibility to make all decisions without including ideas or input from others—even if those children are adults! Ignoring the perceived needs of family members can lead to the excluded ones feeling invisible, not heard, or not understood.

As a parent, I (Kirsten) recently got into a conversation with a friend over summer camps. She was incredibly frustrated with me because I had made the "mistake" of asking my kids what classes they wanted to take rather than just enrolling them in the same classes she had enrolled her kids. My kids were interested in very different classes, and I felt I was being blamed because her kids wouldn't want to go to summer camp if my kids weren't in the same class. "Why would you give them a choice? They are kids. They don't know what they want!" was her response to me. I know she is not alone in this thinking, and I am guilty of making choices for my kids that they are more than capable of making. Who are we as parents to think that we know more about what our kids want than they do if we aren't curious about understanding them? In the same way, how can we expect them to make smart choices if we never include them in the decision-making process?

A few days later, my seven-year-old logged into our Amazon Prime account and ordered toys for him and his sister without asking. After learning what had happened, I asked him why he did it. He said that my husband and I use Amazon all the time for purchases, so why couldn't he and his sister? We sat down and discussed it, explaining that we needed to be included in the process of him (a) using a computer and (b) making purchases. As parents, we expect and want our kids to include us in every aspect of their lives, yet we are quick to exclude our kids in so many situations without even thinking about it—it's faster, it's easier, and it controls the outcome parents want. When we asked our son how he thought we should handle his Amazon purchases, he came up with a plan to make back the money, which included a consequence for buying without permission—both of which were much more onerous than either my husband or I would have ever suggested. It was an interesting process to watch and one that he owned.

An added value of this curious approach is the introduction of accountability. When using an exclusive approach, there is little opportunity for anyone to be accountable for outcomes, since they were not involved in the decision process. With an inclusive approach, accountability can be introduced with outcomes defined and agreed to.

We recognize many parents feel they are the "boss" of their children, preferring an exclusive, power-over approach, particularly when dealing with situations where they feel discipline is needed. We recognize this is a hot spot for many. We have also experienced the value of a more inclusive approach as a parent and a child.

I (Kathy) know when Kirsten was a child, sometimes I was exclusive in my decision making, and sometimes I was inclusive. I learned that inclusion was the more effective strategy. For one thing, how long does a parent hold the exclusive position, being better and/or smarter than their child? When a child graduates with a PhD or is the CEO of a company, is the parent still the exclusive one? When does this positional transition occur?

When I was a young occupational therapist, another therapist shared her perspective that all children were little people—real people who needed to be treated with respect, which included listening to their perspectives and seeking to understand their needs and wants. Although I know I sometimes did not understand my kids as much as I should have, I tried to be inclusive—seeking their input, answering their questions, and trying to recognize their wisdom and insights while keeping them safe and protected.

Shifting from One Perspective to Diverse Perspectives

There are approximately six billion people on this planet, and every one of us has our own unique perspective based on our experiences. Sometimes our perspective appears to be the same as another's, but when we become curious and dig deeper, we learn that the rational evidence that supports their perspective may be different than ours. Under the old paradigm, people assumed their perspectives were the only ones, a mindset reinforced by a top-down leadership model that prioritized the perspective of the person in power.

In the flatter, more transparent Information Age, we can no longer assume everyone thinks and experiences life as we do. We are beginning to recognize that everyone has their own perspective and to welcome the diversity of thought that results. When we think only of our own perspective, how can we begin to understand others? We are not saying anyone needs to give up his or her perspective. We can hold onto our own perspective, value it as correct for us, *and* appreciate the different perspective of others. We can disagree with their perspective. We can also learn from their perspective and what supports it.

Although we may think we appreciate diverse perspectives, we often learn otherwise when our perspective clashes with another. For example, a supervisor of a shipping department has been loading and unloading for twenty-five years. According to her perspective, when unloading items upon arrival, the smallest should be unloaded first because they are easier to lift, and the heavy ones should be left to the end. Once the heaviest item is unloaded, the truck is able to leave. They then move the items to a pallet, with the smaller ones loaded on top, before the forklift is used to move them all into the storage area.

A newer employee starts to unload, taking the heaviest item first and putting it directly on the pallet, and then moves the smaller items on top so the pallet is then ready to be moved by the forklift into storage. If the supervisor believes her perspective is the only one, she may correct the new employee and ask him to complete the task the way she thinks it should be completed—perhaps because it has always been done that way. On the other hand, the new employee may see the supervisor's method as inefficient and become frustrated at having to complete an extra step in the process.

However, if the newer employee becomes curious, understanding that his perspective is not the only one, he may discover that the supervisor learned this method when they had older, fragile pallets and needed to get everything off the delivery truck quickly. Likewise, if the supervisor becomes curious about the employee's perspective, she may discover that this additional step may not be needed now that they have newer, stronger pallets. Together they could come up with a different approach that could be both effective and efficient.

If we want to have respectful conversations that support collaboration, innovation, understanding, and strong relationships, then we must be curious about the perspectives of others. Once we understand the perspectives of others, we can begin to find common ground from which we can seek to build collaboration that works for all concerned.

How to Be Curious

Along with our clients, we have experienced the benefits and power of curiosity. When we hear that employees and supervisors do not feel listened to or understood, we begin by teaching them the three Curiosity Skills:

1. Be present to ABSORB the speaker's message
2. Choose how to listen
3. Ask curious open questions

Together these skills form a communication strategy that can be used every day in conversations to enhance awareness, improve interactions, encourage collaboration, and create a non-blaming culture focused on continual learning—all of which lead to stronger relationships built on trust. Employees begin to feel seen, heard, and understood.

This strategy also transfers well to the home, supporting effective connections in which both children and parents feel understood at any age. When we seek to understand others, we are validating them and making them feel visible, which can be powerful, particularly for children. In the next three chapters, we are going to teach you these three Curiosity Skills so you too can reap the benefits.

CHAPTER 2

BE PRESENT

With the past, I have nothing to do; nor with the future. I live now.
Ralph Waldo Emerson

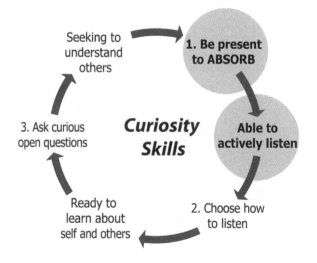

R ecently, I (Kirsten) attended a Mindful Leadership Workshop at UCLA. At the beginning of the workshop, we did an exercise to see how present we were in our daily activities. As I went through the questionnaire, it became clear how much I was missing. I thought I was being a stealth Jedi, always one step ahead so I could accomplish the millions of tasks needed to complete the day successfully. I had done yoga and meditation; I felt I knew how to be present. But staring back at me on the questionnaire was anything but stealth Jedi behavior. I had, in fact, forgotten the number-one rule of a Jedi: be present.

As I sat back and reflected on this, I had a huge "aha" moment about how my lack of presence was impacting my kids' lives. If we aren't present, we can't be curious. One of my favorite things about my kids is that they are constantly present and consistently curious; they don't know how to be any different—yet! And here I am, pulling them out of the moment by constantly rushing them to the next thing, never giving them the time or space to be present, to be curious, to self-reflect, or to discover. If parents are the first influencers of leadership and leadership styles, what am I modeling to my kids?

In our busy lives, most of us aren't even aware of how distracted we are. Such distractions interfere with our abilities to nurture relationships and create repercussions for us as leaders, parents, or colleagues. As we think about what we need to pick up on the way home, e-mails we need to answer, meetings we need to schedule, what we are going to have for dinner, or the million things we want to do and haven't done—all while trying to have a conversation with someone—we are not present and therefore can't fully listen.

As a working mom, I (Kathy) know that I had many things on my mind every moment. I was distracted so easily and found I rarely dedicated my full attention to anything or anyone. Over the years, I have learned the errors of my ways. Once I learned to truly listen to another person and give them my full attention, I realized how easily two people can establish a connection based on understanding. It all begins with choosing to be present.

Choosing to Be Present

Being present is a choice we all have every minute of every day. Some would argue that it is the most important choice we can make – to be present in the moment and aware of the here and now. When you think about it, when you aren't present in the moment, you are never fully experiencing your external and internal worlds. If you are never truly here or there, what kind of life are you living? What kind of relationships are you building? Most importantly, what kind of understanding of self and others are your cultivating?

For us, being present means focusing on the here and now. When we are present, we are not thinking about what we did an hour ago or what we need to be doing next; we're focused on what is happening right now. This can be much easier said than done. In fact, right now as you are reading, you may find yourself thinking about other things you need to do, should be doing, or want to be doing, indicating that you are not fully present in the moment.

To be present requires that we turn off the chatter in our heads, freeing ourselves of what may have happened in the past or anticipating what will happen in the future. It requires us to be in a highly aware state. Take a moment and think about how you feel when you're listening to music you really love and get lost in the moment, or when you're reading a book and get lost in the words on the page. Think about when you're walking in the forest or visiting an art gallery, and you only notice your surroundings. You are present, aware of only what is going on right now. Being present helps us find a place of calm where we feel grounded, can be at peace with ourselves, and attend to what is happening in this moment. It is also the only way we can access curiosity and intentionally listen to someone who is speaking to us.

Be Present and ABSORB

In our distracted, time-constrained world, we need to bring ourselves into the moment and focus on truly listening, or ABSORBing, what is being said to us. Setting an intention to ABSORB ensures we become present and remain in the moment to listen, which is the first of our Curiosity Skills. ABSORB stands for:

A—Attention
B—Body Language and Tone of Voice
S—Stop and Focus
O—Open to Understanding, Not Judging
R—Repeat through Paraphrase
B—Becalm the Gremlins

Attention

Most of us understand that there is a difference between hearing and listening. *Hearing* is the perception of sensory data received by the ear and transmitted to the brain, where the data is translated into identifiable sounds. *Listening* means paying attention to these sounds. We may not always be able to choose what we hear, yet we can always choose whether we're paying attention to it—whether it's the birds chirping outside or a coworker's conversation.

Right now, as I (Kathy) am writing, I hear my young grandson, who has just been put to bed, crying. I can also hear other noises around me—voices in the rest of the house and voices in boats in front of our house. I can choose to pay attention to certain noises in order to merely identify them, pay attention to them so I can listen to them, or ignore them so they remain background noise. When I choose to pay attention to my grandson crying, I listen to the quality of his cry, recognize his frustration because he does not want to go to sleep, and know he will soon be asleep. I am paying attention to him—*listening* to him—and choosing to ignore (hence, only hear) all the other voices around me.

When we are in a conversation and give someone our full attention, we are present and actively ready to listen without distraction. We think of attention as a state of readiness to be in a conversation, something that is needed if we are going to actively listen to what the speaker is saying and become curious about understanding them. Most of us have no awareness of the level of attention we give (or fail to give) when we listen, and instead find ourselves distracted by the thoughts of the past or future, feelings of tiredness or hunger, or the noises of our environment, all of which compete with our ability to be present.

A person can only pay attention to one thing at a time. So the first step to being present in conversation is to choose to give the speaker your full attention and suspend all other thoughts or distractions. Once you make this choice, you will begin to actively listen to what the speaker has to say, rather than just passively hear it.

Some of our clients, upon realizing they have been distracted in conversation, have found it useful to snap their fingers or pinch themselves to "snap out of it," bringing their attention to the here and now and allowing them to actively choose to pay attention to the speaker and listen.

Body Language and Tone of Voice

When fully present and paying attention, we are fully aware of verbal and nonverbal cues. Verbal cues include the spoken words themselves, while nonverbal cues include other elements of communication such as body language and tone of voice. We have learned that lack of congruency between the two can lead to misunderstandings, conflict, and fractured relationships.

In his study of human communication, UCLA professor emeritus of psychology Albert Mehrabian found that, when attitudes and feelings are involved, 7 percent of a message is conveyed through the words that are spoken, 38 percent in the way the words are spoken, and 55 percent through facial expressions and gestures.[5]

For example, let's say someone purses their lips, crosses their arms emphatically, and says in a brusque tone: "Her comments did not bother me at all." What message are you receiving from this person? As the listener in this conversation, you understand the message of the verbal cues, but the nonverbal cues—the person's tone of voice, facial expression, and body language—signal a very different message than the words spoken. When emotions have come into play for the speaker, the messages of the spoken words and the nonverbal cues will often lack congruency, which can be confusing for the listener. Since nonverbal cues present 93 percent of the message, we will most likely pay attention to the nonverbal cues. Most of us have observed the co-worker or the spouse who, when asked to do something they don't especially like to do, reacts with a tone of voice or a controlled facial expression that clearly communicates this person is upset and not happy to comply. All cues help us to understand the true message the speaker is attempting to convey.

The lack of congruency between verbal and nonverbal cues isn't limited to adults; we've all seen young children behave in this way when they first exhibit nonverbal cues. They stomp their feet and cross their arms, and when asked, "What's wrong?" reply, "Nothing." They may stomp off, burst into tears, throw something, or even hit someone. Their emotions may have taken over, which can result in conflict and confusion. They simply don't know what to do next. As adults, we can recognize that these young children are overcome with emotion by reading their nonverbal cues. The challenge for us is in "listening" to the children, so we can understand what they are trying to communicate to us.

In my (Kirsten's) coaching career, I've learned how important it is to be able to authentically express oneself at all times. Our lack of expression can cost us our relationships with friends, family, and clients; it can even cost us our jobs. I have also learned that the reason so many of us are unable to express ourselves is that we have never been taught how. How often do you struggle with self-expression? I know I still struggle with it, especially as the mother of two young children. I have learned that how we learn to cope with our emotions as kids influences our coping skills (or lack thereof) as we become adults and leaders. If we have no awareness of our body language or congruency of expression when we get emotional, then it is challenging to "listen" to it and understand it in others.

We have all had conversations with people who don't make eye contact, who don't face us, who fold their arms, or who communicate in some way that they are not actually listening to us—indicating they aren't with us in the moment. How does an employee feel when his supervisor uses her body language in this way? Pretty vulnerable. He may begin to wonder if he is about to be disciplined or even fired. Anxiety sets in, and sidebar conversations begin to occur with colleagues, resulting in lost productivity and engagement.

Stop and Focus

In the midst of our demanding lives, we are expected (by ourselves and others) to complete myriad tasks—sometimes simultaneously!—within a limited timeframe, challenging our ability to be present. In the midst of performing these tasks, someone in our lives may need our attention. They may have a question, they may need our advice or direction, or they may just want an opinion, and we are reluctant to drop what we're doing and take the time to listen. We continue with our own activity— cooking, texting, watching a TV show—while "listening" to the person.

In the end, we find we don't do either task very well. We forget to add a key ingredient to a dish we are preparing, we make errors as we text that oh-so-important message, we miss an actor's punchline—and we don't understand what the person is saying to us while we're otherwise engaged because we aren't present and haven't listened.

If you ask a parent what is more important to them—spending time with their kids or ticking off items on their "to do" list—most will choose spending time with their kids. Similarly, most leaders will say it's important to spend time talking with those who report to them, as well as with their colleagues and clients. We've come to recognize that, if leaders take time out of their schedule to talk to employees, clients, or associates, or parents take time to be with their kids, they often feel guilty for not completing their obligations. How often have you checked your e-mail, texts, or social media when spending time with your kids or colleagues so you don't *miss* anything? So, while we understand the value and importance of relationship building, what is it that prompts people to behave in opposition to that understanding? Why does our society place more importance on task completion? And what price does one pay when sacrificing presence and personal connection for the sake of a task?

I (Kathy) find it interesting how little parents truly listen to their children, particularly when the children are young, choosing to do many things while "listening" to what their kids have to say. How present are they when with their kids? I am also intrigued at how these same parents then complain about their teens who don't listen to them. I think these teens have had great role models when it comes to not being present and not intentionally listening. No wonder they don't listen once they are old enough to have figured out how to multitask, are on their phones connecting 24/7, and involved in their own teen world.

If we want to try to understand what others are saying to us, we need to be present and focus on them. To focus means to stop multitasking, stop task completion, and intentionally bring your attention to the speaker. This is how we actively listen to someone; this is how we convey respect in wanting to understand what they are saying.

Of course, it sounds great in theory. But what happens when you have a deadline or need to complete a thought, and are interrupted by someone who needs to talk now? Perhaps you're a supervisor with an open-door policy, and one of your employees walks into your office while you're responding to an urgent e-mail. You need to finish the message and can't afford to lose your train of thought, so you don't stop writing, and you don't acknowledge the employee when she enters, not knowing that she needs a piece of information from you to complete her work. In this moment, both of you are feeling overwhelmed and misunderstood.

In our workshops, we've been asked by those in both roles how to handle this situation. Through our own experiences in similar circumstances and feedback from others, we've discovered a straightforward solution: if we don't have enough time to stop, be present, and listen, we can schedule a meeting at a mutually agreed-upon time, so we can focus on what the other person wants to say to us. Asking for the time necessary to complete an e-mail, make a phone call, or finish a task before engaging in conversation shows that we want to actively listen to the other person. We know when we stop and focus, we are seeking to understand them and showing our respect for others, honoring their desire or need to communicate with us.

If someone indicates a need for our attention in that moment, we as the listener can stop long enough to determine how to accommodate his or her urgent request. Again, we are sending the message that we want to listen to them, and we want to focus on what they have to say. We have found that when a request is urgent, it typically takes very little time to address once we stop doing everything else and focus on them.

The strategy is simple: if we are in the midst of completing a task that we don't want to interrupt, we will ask, "How much time do you need?" If the response is, "Five minutes," and we can be interrupted for that much time, we agree to stop what we're doing, focus, and actively listen for five minutes. If the issue isn't resolved after focusing fully for five minutes, we'll say, "This seems to be more complicated than first thought. I really want to understand your issue, and I'd like to schedule more time for discussion. Let's find an hour later today when I'll have the time to really understand what's going on for you." We know that just because people say they have an open-door policy, it doesn't mean they are available at all times. Rather, it means people are open to scheduling time to be available for others so they can be fully present to see, hear, and understand them.

Open to Understanding, Not Judging

When we are fully present, we are more likely to be open to understand others rather than judge. Being open to understanding others means our focus is on the speaker, we're suspending our judgment, and we're listening to understand them. If we are seeking to understand someone, we need to be open to what they are saying. If we listen to their words and then judge them, how does this help us understand them? We don't think one can seek to understand and judge at the same time. It is one or the other.

I (Kirsten) am fortunate to have a great relationship with my mother. She is always present, taking the time to listen to me without being judgmental or trying to fix things; she just listens. I feel seen, I feel heard, and I feel understood. I want my kids to have the same feeling in their relationship with me. It's freeing. It's respectful, empowering. It makes you feel valued. And this is the biggest realization I've had in my coaching career: everyone wants to be seen, heard, and understood by others, and being open and non-judging is a very important step in achieving this.

In retrospect, I didn't appreciate the importance of presence or listening until I became trained as an executive coach and then became a parent. I had always believed I was good at both. In reality, I was a "fixer." I loved hearing people's stories and helping them fix whatever needed fixing (or what I felt they needed to fix). It made me feel like a valuable friend, to tell them what to do under the guise of "listening." In reality, I was only hearing what I wanted to, when I wanted to, judging their words so I could fix their problem, providing a solution that showed my ability to solve their problems.

When we judge, we close ourselves to possibility. We think we know what is being said, and we listen to the words with our bias, our predetermined outcome already developed. When we judge others, we are holding them up to our perspectives and beliefs and determining they are either better or lesser than us. How does this foster connection and understanding?

When we stop judging and open ourselves to the speaker's perspective, we can begin to connect with the speaker in a way that fosters understanding and creates a better relationship. In short, we open ourselves to possibility.

Repeat through Paraphrase

Organizational consultant Gervase Bushe says in his book *Clear Leadership*, "Paraphrasing back what people are saying forces you to pay attention, not let your mind wander, and ensures that you understand the meaning, not just the words, of what others are saying."[6]

Paraphrasing involves recalling what you've heard the person say, observing their nonverbal cues before responding, and repeating the message using your own words. When we paraphrase back to the speaker, we convey we are paying attention to what the speaker has said, which provides the speaker with the opportunity to gain clarity about what he or she is communicating, and with reassurance that we as the listener are genuinely trying to understand what the speaker is saying.

For example, someone might say to you, "I have so much work to do and I'm not sure how I'll get it all done. I'd hoped to get away this weekend . . . now, I think that's not going to happen." As the listener, you could paraphrase by saying, "It sounds like you're disappointed and a bit overwhelmed because of your workload. You'd planned to go away this weekend, and now you think you may have to work."

Paraphrasing is also a useful tool when you find your mind wandering off and thinking about other things rather than listening to the speaker. When you find yourself losing focus, paraphrase back what you think you heard the speaker say to bring your awareness to the present moment. This will help you keep your focus on the here and now and will confirm how much you are actually listening to.

As parents and grandparents, we've found paraphrasing to be a useful tool to mitigate our overwhelming desire to fix or solve everything for our kids, especially in those times when they want nothing more than to be heard.

When picking up my kids from school, I (Kirsten) will ask them how their day has been; occasionally, they will tell me about an uncomfortable event. "Sarah pushed me to the ground and laughed. I hate it when she does that. She's not a friend." Instinctively, I want to make the situation "right." I hear my daughter is upset, and I want to make her feel better. If I say, "I'm sure it was an accident. Sarah is your friend and she probably didn't mean to do it," this answer just makes her mad. If I say, "That was mean of Sarah. What did you do so she would want to push you to the ground?" I am judging both of them, with a hint of blame and shame. My kid is upset and hurt, and she doesn't want to be friends with someone who has done something she doesn't like—and rightly so. She is not asking for a solution; she just wants to be heard by sharing her experience with me.

A paraphrased response would be, "It sounds like you were hurt and angry when Sarah pushed you to the ground and laughed, and you don't want to be friends with someone who treats you this way." Paraphrasing allows us to let our children know we are fully present listening to them, without jumping to solve the problem. In any context, paraphrasing supports understanding and can communicate empathy.

In *The 8th Habit*, author Stephen R. Covey's model for conflict resolution, "The Third Alternative Communication," uses paraphrasing in its practice. His experience indicates that when one person shares his or her perspective, and the other person completes his or her paraphrase in a way that allows the first person to feel understood, most conflicts can be resolved.[7]

We think of paraphrasing as an art form, and we offer an exercise in our workshops that allows participants to become familiar with the technique.

Paraphrasing Exercise with Partner: Choose a partner. One person takes the role of storyteller, and talks on any topic for one minute (or two, or five, if you're up for the challenge), after which the partner paraphrases back what he or she has heard. The storyteller then provides feedback on the accuracy of the paraphrase. Now switch roles.

What was it like to listen so you could paraphrase back what you heard? How accurate were you?

We have found that participants realize very quickly how difficult it is to both truly listen and then repeat back the story they have heard in their own words. Once you feel comfortable paraphrasing, think about how you can incorporate these enhanced listening skills into your life.

For those who want to experiment with paraphrasing on your own first, here is an exercise you can try individually whenever you want:

Individual Exercise: When having a conversation and listening to a co-worker, friend, or loved one, take the time to paraphrase back what you heard them say. "It sounds like" or "what I am hearing is" are great ways to gain clarity and let the speaker feel heard. It is also an opportunity for the speaker to clarify if, in fact, what you are paraphrasing is not what he or she was trying to say.

What do you notice about how you are listening?

How are your conversations different?

What have you learned when paraphrasing?

Becalm the Gremlins

How often do you notice that inner critic in your head who just can't seem to keep quiet? We all have this "gremlin" voice, also known as self-talk, that so often competes for our attention when we're in a conversation with someone we want to listen to. A client once referred to the gremlin in her head as her board of directors, that group of voices that told her what to do, interrupted her, judged her and others, and generally got in the way of her commitment to focus.

That voice can be quite distracting, sabotaging our ability to be present and focus on what is being said. If we allow the gremlins to take control, our eyes glaze over, our body language becomes more passive, and before we know it, listening stops. As we all know by now, poor listening results in lost connection and missed opportunities.

A client of ours, a physician working on his communication skills, decided that the voices in his head were constantly scrutinizing his "to do" list. He imagined they were ensuring he wouldn't forget the things he was supposed to do. He was able to lower the volume of the "voices" while at work. However, when his kids were competing for his attention as a listener at home, he sometimes found himself distracted by his thoughts about the tasks he needed to tend to the next day and was unable to be fully present. Once he realized this, he decided to keep an actual "to do" list for the next day's work, as well as an "action" list that contained all the long-term tasks he knew he was responsible for completing. He reckoned he'd need to spend a certain amount of time each evening updating his "to do" list for the next day, and moving the items from his "action" list to his "to do" list when appropriate. Once these lists were in place, he could trust that he would not overlook any of his responsibilities. He could then turn off the internal chatter and devote his attention to being present and actively listening to his family and friends.

Being Present to ABSORB Supports Active Listening

As people put their first Curiosity Skill into practice and choose to be fully present and ABSORB what others are saying, they begin to have a different experience in their conversations, learning more about the person speaking to them. Sometimes others even thank them for listening! When we are fully present and actively listen to others, we create an experience for listeners that can evolve into a powerful learning experience for them as well. They may even become converts, beginning to intentionally and actively listen to others themselves.

Kirsten and I (Kathy) have talked a lot about our experiences of being present so we can listen, how we try to listen actively whenever someone is speaking to us. When I began the process of learning to be present so I could listen, I found it was exhausting; being present and ABSORBing every word spoken by another person was hard—really hard! With time and practice, it became easier, and it's now instinctual for me.

Now I know when I am in the moment and really listening to someone—when Kirsten wants to share an experience, or my husband wants to share about his day—because I completely connect with them. I feel grounded, respectful of them, and somehow aligned with them. I really love this feeling; I feel suspended in time and space. If I stop being present and listening, I'm just as aware of that. I'm no longer grounded, I'm not connected to the person in the same way, and I'm sure they know I've tuned them out. In that moment, I feel

I am not valuing them; I'm being disrespectful to them, and it's not a feeling I enjoy.

I am also acutely aware of when others aren't present and listening to me—I don't enjoy that, either! I tend to shut down when I don't feel the person is listening to what I am saying, and my desire to talk is diminished. As a colleague once said after she'd learned this first Curiosity Skill, "Once you are present and actively listening, you can never go back."

Creating relationships where others feel listened to is powerful for all concerned. Imagine your children thanking you for being present, listening to them, knowing you want to see, hear, and understand them. Being the role model for your children can create the early influences that will support them in becoming people who understand the experience of listening and being listened to.

But there's more to listening than just choosing to be present and ABSORBing what others are saying. We'll talk more specifically about *how* you can choose to listen to what you ABSORB, and how each of these Listening Choices influences your leadership, your relationships, and your outcomes.

Take Action

1. When we do the same (or similar) routine every day, it can be easy to operate on autopilot—missing experiences, taking relationships for granted, or not applying yourself 100 percent. Whenever something becomes a habit, it is easy to stop being mindful about it or aware of it. For one day, try switching up your routine and see what you notice. Take a different route to work, try a new approach to solving a challenge, have lunch at a new place, or better yet, take a lunch break and actually leave your workspace. What do you notice?

2. As you enter your conversations, set an intention to be curious and learn one new thing about the person you are speaking to—even if it is someone you have known your whole life. Ground yourself in the here and now, use your Curiosity Skills to ABSORB what the speaker is saying, and see what you learn.

3. As you go throughout your day, pay attention to how your negative self-talk, or what we call the "gremlins" in your head, also competes for your attention in the present moment. Pay attention to what those gremlins are saying, and consider how you can quiet them. What can you do to acknowledge them and thereby dim the noise, creating silence to focus on the here and now? When you do, what do you notice? How do you feel? How long can you stay in this place of silence?

4. Practicing being present in the moment for just one minute helps, and the more you practice, the more you will find yourself living in silence, being in that sweet spot called now where all that matters is what is going on in the moment. Become fully aware of what being present means to you, so when you enter into a conversation, you can easily access this place and ABSORB what the speaker is saying.

CHAPTER 3

CHOOSE HOW TO LISTEN

The most basic of all human needs is the need to understand and be understood. The best way to understand people is to listen to them.
Ralph Nichols, Founding member of the
International Listening Association

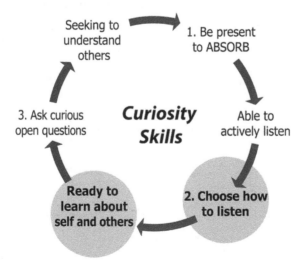

A few years ago, we were working with a leader of an organization who was extremely frustrated with her team. Team morale was low, jobs weren't being done effectively, and gossip and judging amongst team members were influencing the team's performance and organizational culture. Her team wasn't doing what she thought she was asking them to do, and it was becoming a huge problem for their organization. Our client felt like she was being disrespected as the leader, and she was fed up.

When we met with the team members, they too were frustrated. They felt they were working hard to meet almost impossible expectations. Breaks weren't scheduled in a way that made sense for them, with many feeling like they had no break for lunch or even using the restroom. They all felt their team leader wasn't listening to *them* and intentionally wanted them to fail. Why would they want to work hard for someone who wanted them to fail?

We sat down with the team leader and got curious. It sounded like listening was an issue on both sides, and we wanted to understand what was standing in the way. No one's needs were being met, all at the expense of the clients of their organization. But as we talked to our client about listening to the needs of her team, she became confused. As the leader of the organization, she believed that it was her role to tell her team what to do because the leader was supposed to know what was best for her team. "How do you know what is best for your team if you don't listen to what they need?" we asked. Our client had never considered it.

As we dug deeper to understand what "listening" meant to our client, she had a revelation. She felt she had never been listened to—as a child, a team member, or a leader. Because she didn't know what being listened to felt like, she didn't know how to listen to others. Our client had, in fact, been raised with that old hierarchical belief that leaders make the decisions for their teams, and if you listen to others or ask questions, you must not know what is best for your team and therefore are not a strong leader. Fearful of not being respected as a strong leader, our client kept choosing not to listen to her team and their needs, telling them instead what she thought was best for them based on her own perspective.

The Importance of *How* We Listen

In the first Curiosity Skill, being present to ABSORB, we learned that listening begins with the choice to pay attention to what the speaker is saying. But there's more to listening than simply choosing to pay attention. *How* are we listening to them? Are we listening for full understanding, to hear what we want to hear, or to judge? What are we thinking as we ABSORB what they're saying?

Most of us are never taught how to listen for understanding. We intuitively began listening in utero and honed this ability as babies, most likely as a survival skill to make sure we could connect with our caregivers and have our needs met. As we matured, listening was just an expectation of life, helping us connect with others to learn, express ourselves, understand, and build relationships.

Listening is, in fact, fundamental to how we communicate; it may be the single most important skill we use. How we listen affects every choice we make, every relationship we build, and at some level, everything we do: our interactions with employees and colleagues, our conduct in meetings, our social engagements, and our responses in a job interview. Our failure to listen well to others can lead to fractured relationships and an inability to meet even basic objectives.

Many of us take the act of listening for granted, believing we're good listeners. Yet when we ask others how often they feel listened to, most will say rarely; no one we've asked has said they feel listened to all the time. When others are not listening to them, they're aware of it and find it frustrating; some go so far as to say they feel disrespected. When we ask how often they listen to others, they admit they, too, fall short; many times, they can't recall what others have shared with them. How often do you feel others actively listen to you, wanting to understand what you are saying? How often do you listen this way with others?

The Five Listening Choices

If we want to understand the perspectives of others, to be respectful of them, we need to intentionally choose *how* we listen to them. When we are fully present in the moment, ABSORBing what is being said to us, all of a sudden several listening choices become available to us. Rather than simply two listening choices—i.e., whether to listen or not—we believe we actually have *five* listening choices whenever we are listening to another person. For example, we may choose to listen in order to understand the full intended meaning of the speaker. We may choose to just listen to the words spoken. Or we may choose not to listen, ignoring the speaker completely. Again, the choice is ours.

Each choice has its appropriate time and place, and the key is to be intentional, selecting the choice that is most useful and respectful in the situation. Not all five choices of listening foster curiosity, and hence not all five choices support being present and ABSORBing the message of the speaker (the first Curiosity Skill) or responding with curious open questions (the third Curiosity Skill, which you'll learn about in chapter 4).

As we go through the five listening choices, we invite you to think about what choice resonates for you and why. We also invite you to be open to new ways of listening. Experiment with all five choices in order to understand how you typically listen, and to choose how you want to listen moving forward.

Listening Choice 1: Ignore the Speaker

In Choice 1, we are choosing not to listen to the speaker. We may hear noise, but rather than actively listening to it, we are compiling a to-do list, thinking about a plan for later, reading e-mails/social media posts, or waiting for the speaker to be silent so we can change the subject to speak about what we want. In short, we are not present, and we are not paying attention. In Choice 1, we have no opportunity to be curious, and the "listener" may be seen as disrespecting the speaker. An alternative choice the "listener" has in some situations is to excuse himself from the conversation.

Value of Choice 1: Choice 1 is useful when we need to escape a conversation, and even though we know we may be seen as disrespectful for choosing this option, it is the choice that is most helpful in the moment. Perhaps we are sitting next to a "chatty Patty" on a plane, and although we have indicated we would prefer not to get to know our seatmate, the companion continues to talk and talk. This choice can also be useful when focused on completing a project, watching a game, or engaged in an activity, and we don't want to be disturbed (and perhaps have had to repeatedly remind others of this fact). Therefore, we may choose not to listen to anyone who happens to speak to us.

Listening Choice 2: Focus on Me

In Choice 2, we choose to pay attention to the speaker through the lens of the gremlin, or that inner critic inside our head, which compares the perspective of the speaker with our own and judges the speaker in the context of us. Like Choice 1, Choice 2 gives us no opportunity to be curious, as our thoughts are focused on our needs rather than those of the speaker.

Here's what Choice 2 might look like in a personal conversation:

Speaker: "I think I will stop dating John."
Listener thinks: *About time. I would never have gone out with John in the first place.*

The comment is heard in a way that puts it in the context of the listener.

In the workplace, Choice 2 might look like this:

Speaker (Leader): "I want those reports on my desk by Friday."
Listener thinks: *Great. I have to work extra hard to get the reports in by Friday, and I know they won't be read until next week. This will create added pressure for me. I wanted to leave early on Thursday, and now I won't be able to.*

Value of Choice 2: In our workshops, discussion about Choice 2 typically moves to the topic of friends and family. Listening with intention can be hard work, and we don't necessarily have to choose to work that hard all the time. It has been suggested that when sitting around, chatting over a glass of wine with a girlfriend or relative, people like to judge each other and think about what is being said as if it were happening to them. They are relaxed and enjoying themselves, and everyone is showing up the same way—everyone is listening, laughing, and just having fun hanging out together. Everyone already feels connected to and supported by each other, and they don't necessarily need to feel completely understood at all times.

However, some people also choose Choice 2 when they engage in judgmental self-talk, which can spiral down into negativity, inadequacy, and feeling not good enough.

Finally, Choice 2 may be used when we are asked for our opinion, expert or otherwise. We listen to what is being said, put ourselves in the place of the speaker, and provide an opinion based on how we think we would feel and what we would do if we were in their place. We draw on our own knowledge and judgment when thinking about our response. This choice is often used by mentors, advisors, and consultants who rely on their own expertise, experience, and knowledge to create their judgment before they provide their opinion. The listener can thus choose to control the outcome of the conversation through their responses, which provide clear advice and can bring the conversation to a conclusion.

Listening Choice 3: Focus on You

In Choice 3, as the listener, we pay attention to the speaker, and our "gremlin voice" judges the speaker in the speaker's own context. Choice 3 is frequently the choice of helpers, or people who want to support others by providing advice and helping them to solve problems. They pay attention to what is being said and jump to thinking about a solution, judging the speaker's situation and telling him or her what to do, even if advice is not requested.

Using the same examples as used in Choice 2, Choice 3 listening would look like this:

Speaker: "I think I will stop dating John."
Listener thinks: *About time. He has not treated you well, and you should have stopped dating him long ago. In fact, you should never have dated him in the first place.*

Or in the workplace:

Speaker (Leader): "I want those reports on my desk by Friday."
Listener thinks: *Great. Why does she need the reports by Friday? She is going golfing Friday afternoon, so she won't check them until Monday. She is so selfish and doesn't understand anything.*

Value of Choice 3: As with Choice 2, Choice 3 is commonly used in social situations, talks with friends, and parents' interactions with children. Some people enjoy this choice, finding it funny and entertaining. We frequently listen to comedians and sitcoms using Choices 2 and 3 in response to their attempt at humor that is self-deprecating, disparaging of others, or blaming of self or others. It is interesting that so much of the humor depicted in our society is created at the expense of the speaker or others.

Sometimes Choice 3 has its advantages. Similar to Choice 2, professionals are expected to use their judgment to develop a solution for the client and can think about the solution before providing advice about what is best for the client moving forward.

Listening Choice 4: Focus on Understanding

In Choice 4, we choose to relinquish control over the outcome of the conversation. We intentionally, actively listen to what is being said and how it is said. We do not judge, and our gremlin voice is quiet. Instead we are receptive and open to the speaker, seeking to understand what the speaker is saying. We have no preconceived ideas about the outcome or what we think the speaker should do. We have the opportunity to be curious, to explore possibilities.

Looking at our two examples from above:

Speaker: "I think I will stop dating John."
Listener thinks: *I wonder what has made her decide to do this? How is she going to do this? How does she feel about this decision?*

Or in the workplace:

Speaker (Leader): "I want those reports on my desk by Friday."
Listener thinks: *Given the amount of work this will entail, I wonder how I can achieve this? She will be out of the office Friday afternoon. What is her reason for this deadline? How does she think I can do this?*

Value of Choice 4: Judging is absent from Choice 4 listening. One's judging gremlin voice is silent, and the listener is open, curious, inquisitive, taking no responsibility for the outcome of the conversation. The listener wants to better understand the speaker's perspective and intention.

The listener can also begin to empathize with the speaker if appropriate, as seen in the first example when the listener thinks, "How does she feel about this decision?" *Empathy* is the ability to figuratively move towards the other person and appreciate what that person is feeling. It is a valuable tool when attempting to understand another, as it builds connection and deepens relationships.

This choice has great value in creating an open space for exploration and inquisitive thinking, allowing the listener to focus on the speaker. Having surrendered control over the outcome, the listener may find this choice frustrating due to a lack of direction. If the listener feels a need to be more involved or attached to the outcome, Choice 5 may be a better option (see below).

Choice 4 supports accountability on the part of the speaker. It is used a great deal by coaches, mentors, and other professionals who are able to sit in ambiguity, with no need to control the outcome of the conversation, and remain curious about the speaker.

One of our workshop participants shared her experience in using Choice 4 with her elderly grandmother in a care facility. She enjoyed visiting her grandmother, and she noticed that her grandmother would repeat the same stories over and over again, sometimes repeating one that had just been shared. She found herself judging her grandmother for being repetitive and somewhat confused. But when she used Choice 4 listening and intentionally became curious, asking her grandmother open questions related to the story, her grandmother shared greater detail, instead of repeating the same detail over again. She found she stopped judging her grandmother and was no longer invested in the outcome of the conversation, but simply enjoying just being with her grandmother as she learned more about her. She decided she was going to use Choice 4 whenever she was with her grandmother and looked forward to learning more about her life.

Listening Choice 5: Focus on Us

Although completely relinquishing control can create a deep connection, sometimes it does not serve us to be ambiguous when we have a stake in the outcome of the conversation. In Choice 5, we choose to intentionally, actively listen *and* remain invested in the outcome of the conversation. We want to understand the perspectives of others and work together to agree on what to do next.

Looking at our examples:

Speaker: "I think I will stop dating John."
Listener thinks: *I wonder when she plans to speak to John? I will be away this weekend and want to support her. What support does she think she will need? How can I be there for her if I am away?*

So the listener is open and curious *and* is invested in supporting her friend.

Or in the workplace:

Speaker (Leader): "I want those reports on my desk by Friday."
Listener thinks: *I need to leave early on Thursday. How important is the Friday deadline, given she will not be in the office for part of the day? What do I need to do to meet this request and keep to my schedule, leaving early Thursday? I wonder how she would feel about moving this to Monday morning?*

Value of Choice 5: As we remain curious and seek an agreement that will work for both parties, we can be empathetic to the needs of the speaker, building connection and greater understanding. This choice provides the opportunity for accountability moving forward.

This approach is best used when both parties have a stake in the outcome, such as a negotiation, conflict resolution, or collaboration. The listener is open to understanding the perspectives of the speaker while staying invested in the outcome as the conversation unfolds.

The Five Power of Curiosity Listening Choices

Our Listening Choices	What Listener Is Thinking	Characteristics	Uses
Choice 1: Ignore the speaker	Listener ignores what is being said	Does not listen Is closed to all ideas Is silent Not interested in understanding others Focused elsewhere	When listener wants silence When all else has failed when trying to end a conversation When listener does not value building connection When listener desires to shut someone down

Choice 2: Focus on Me	"If I were you, I wouldn't do that." "I want you to . . . ." "I think you should . . . ." "I can't believe you would . . . ."	Listens to pay attention Is closed to ideas of others Judges self Judges others and compares to self Needs to be right or fears being wrong Does not attempt to understand others	When listener wants to share own perspective As a response to the question, "What would you do?" In mentoring and professional advising contexts When hanging out with friends or family In emergency situations
Choice 3: Focus on You	"You should . . . ." "You need to . . . ." "You have to . . . ."	Listens to pay attention Is closed to ideas of others Judges self and others Desires/needs to help (even if no request for help was made) Does not attempt to understand others Offers an expert opinion	When providing advice When providing information, particularly as a professional such as a doctor, lawyer, mentor, or counselor

Choice 4: Focus on Understanding	"How did you do that?" "What would you do?"	Actively listens Is curious Seeks to understand others Does not judge Tests assumptions Allows for ambiguity Demonstrates empathy	When desiring to understand perspectives of others When gaining information When supporting learning In coaching, mentoring, and professional advising contexts
Choice 5: Focus on Us	"I need you to . . ." "How do you think we can achieve this?" "We need to . . ." "What can I do to help you achieve this?"	Actively listens Is curious Describes own interest Is open to perspectives of others Seeks to understand others Creates common ground to move forward Demonstrates empathy Remains invested in the outcome	In negotiation In conflict resolution When collaborating as teams, leaders, parents, etc. When developing goals When supporting others

We believe you always have all five listening choices available to you at any moment—as long as you are present and fully ABSORBing the speaker's message. That means you can even choose to shift from one style of listening to another within the same conversation. For example, the parent of an adult child may be called on to help her son deal with an issue. The parent may choose to listen using Choice 4 (Focus on Understanding) as the son shares his issue, creating empathy and clarity about the situation. She may then move to Choice 5 (Focus on Us) if she has a personal interest in the outcome—for example, ensuring her son is safe and happy. She may at some point move to Choice 3 (Focus on You) or 2 (Focus on Me) as she prepares to provide the requested advice.

The key is to intentionally choose *how* we listen respectfully to build relationships. Your listening choice can create the space for learning, understanding, connection, collaboration, innovation, and inspiration— or it can limit the space to ignoring, judging, and criticizing.

As you have probably noticed from the discussion above, only two of our listening choices—Choices 4 and 5—provide an opportunity for curiosity. If you have made the choice to be curious in your listening approach, then it's time to learn the third Curiosity Skill, which is asking curious open questions. This skill can help you remain open and curious in your understanding as the conversation progresses.

Take Action

Use the chart below to track how you are choosing to listen in conversations. Pay attention to whom you were talking with, how your listening choice influenced the conversation, what the outcome was, and how it affected your relationship.

Cheat Sheet: If you hear yourself saying "I" a lot in conversation, then you are in Choice 2. If you hear yourself saying "you" a lot, then you are in Choice 3. And if you hear yourself asking curious open questions (which you'll learn more about in the next chapter), then you know you are in Choice 4. Practice and play with each choice, and pay attention to the outcomes you achieve. Have fun!

All the charts in the book can be downloaded for free at www. instituteofcuriosity.com.

The 5 Power of Curiosity Listening Choices Tracker

Choice	Who were you talking with? What were you doing?	How did your listening choice influence the conversation/ relationship?	What was the outcome?	What did you learn?	How did it make you feel?
2	Spouse having dinner	We were both frustrated because he wasn't doing what I told him to do	Argument	He doesn't like to do things my way	Angry
5	Discussing project with boss with goal of gaining clarity about how boss wanted project completed	I was present, listened, and asked how I could do it differently— boss was impressed with suggestion and said I got it	New, exciting direction for my project	Once I understood what my boss wanted, I was able to make new suggestions	Excited, invigorated, hopeful

CHAPTER 4

ASK CURIOUS OPEN QUESTIONS

The wise man doesn't give the right answers,
he poses the right questions.
Claude Levi-Strauss

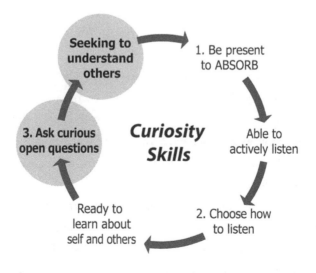

t is late in the afternoon, and a father and his five young kids pile into a subway car. The subway car is pretty full. It is the end of the day, and people are tired, making their way home from work. The father of the kids finds a single seat and sits down. His five kids are visibly frustrated with the number of people around them, and they start pushing one another around, bumping into other passengers. One starts to cry, another gets angry, the third pulls the fourth one's hair, and he screams. They are all upset. The passengers on the subway car stare at the father who has his head in his hands, doing nothing and saying nothing, incredulous he is just ignoring his children.

Appalled by the children's behavior, the passengers in the subway car get frustrated with the kids and the father. One man finally has had enough and snips, "Hey man, you going to wake up and do something about your kids?" The father looks up, agitated, and says, "Cut me some slack; I have had a rough day." You can feel the hair rise on the rest of the passengers. Another says, "Don't be so selfish, man; we have all had a rough day!" As the behavior of the kids escalates, so does the frustration of the passengers. As a passenger on the subway, how would you feel about this situation? What would you want to do?

Now, what if we told you that two days ago, his wife—their mother—was struck by a driver out of nowhere and was killed instantly? He and his children were taking the subway for the first time to her burial. Now, as a passenger, how do you feel about this situation unfolding on the subway? What would you want to do? And how is it different than before?

This story is a popular example used to illustrate how easy it is to judge, criticize, and make assumptions when we aren't curious about understanding someone's perspective. We pass people every day and silently judge them for choices they make that may or may not affect us.

One of the most profound transformations that both of us have experienced in the last ten years has occurred through the use of questions, particularly curious open questions. Asking questions has changed how we think and helped us become more curious and more open in our thought process. Many of our clients have indicated a similar experience. Although they struggled initially with asking rather than telling, as they mindfully set their intention to ask questions, they became more open, non-judging, and generally curious about what others were saying in order to understand them.

Learning to ask questions was really hard for me (Kathy). I grew up in an era where asking questions was frowned upon. If we asked questions, it meant we were trying to challenge the status quo, and as a child, that was not seen as my role. I also recall asking questions meant you didn't know the answer, which could be disastrous as we were expected to know everything or keep quiet. It has only been over the past 10 years, since I have become a coach, that I have felt comfortable asking curious open questions. I have learned that others like to answer questions, and I can see them reflecting on an answer before they respond to my questions. It's fun to watch and even more fun to observe people light up as they share their experiences, their perspectives on things. Even so, I still find it challenging at times!

As children, we are like little sponges, eager to learn and filled with curiosity, asking questions freely (and sometimes really good questions). Yet as adults, so many of us have lost that ability to be curious, that desire to learn more. It is interesting that a two- or three-year-old is quite adept at asking open, curious questions about everything, and yet as adults we typically have little patience for the three-year-old who constantly asks questions that make us think, that take some of our precious time to respond to, that require us to be present in the moment. We need to relearn what used to come so naturally.

Types of Questions

Great leaders, innovative thinkers, and collaborative partners all know new possibilities and opportunities stem from asking a certain type of question. Curiosity is achieved through asking a certain type of question, too. Let's look at some different types of questions and how each type can support you in becoming curious and understanding others.

Closed Questions

Closed questions can be answered with yes or no. As you begin to be mindful about the questions you ask and are asked, you may notice many people expand on the yes or no when responding to closed questions.

Question: Do you want chicken for dinner?
Response: No, I don't think I want chicken. I thought I might pick up sushi on my way home from work.

When one looks at the question asked and the answer provided, the response both answered the question asked and then elaborated upon what the responder did want, even though it was not part of the question. Closed questions can narrow down options (if answered with just yes or no). They support deductive reasoning, that process of elimination where there is a need to narrow down the options and arrive at a choice/solution that seems most viable. In some situations, closed questions are the most appropriate choice.

Question: Will you marry me?
Response: Yes!

Value of Closed Questions: Closed questions shorten or shut down the conversation, which may be valuable in certain contexts. They can narrow the response options as a deductive strategy. And they can also be a good way to check in or confirm a paraphrase made by the listener.

Judging Closed Questions

As the name implies, these are questions generated from judging others and can be answered with yes or no.

Did you screw up and create this mess?

Are you going to continue to be a lazy couch potato forever?

Can you stop daydreaming and pay attention to what I am saying?

Value of Judging Closed Questions: We don't think these questions have much value if there is an intention to be respectful of others. We find people tend to use these questions when being sarcastic or humorous at the expense of another, which is a form of judging.

Curious Open Questions

With curious open questions, the person asking the question does not have an answer and does not intend to judge or blame. Curious open questions promote inductive reasoning, which leads to an expansion of the conversation, where anything goes. They create a sense of possibility, as the answer is not already known. They are questions that cannot be answered with yes or no and typically start with how, who, what, where, when, or why. The term "why" could be perceived as judging, depending on the nonverbal cues used by the person asking the question. For example:

Why would you wear a red dress for your interview?

Depending on where the emphasis is placed, the question can be heard as curious or judging.

Other examples of curious open questions might include:

What was it like to parachute out of a plane?

How can I help you with that?

What can I do differently to better support you?

The Value of Curious Open Questions: Curious open questions allow for ambiguity, where the inquirer suspends his or her need to judge and surrenders control over the direction the conversation may take. They can create a navigational system for a conversation, offering space for reflection that can lead to rich learning. The open space created supports inclusion and engagement and encourages active listening. When we are asked a curious open question, we feel supported and that our perspectives are appreciated. We are welcomed into a place where there is no right or wrong answer and collaboration can thrive, leading to innovation. Believing anything is possible can be really fun for everyone, supporting engagement and resilience.

Leading Open Questions

These questions begin with the same words as curious open questions— how, who, what, where, when, which, and why—but they are not curious because the person asking the question already knows the answer. For example, an instructor may ask a student:

Who is the author of this book?

What era was the book based on?

How many characters were in the book?

Who is the hero of the story?

In this case, the instructor is fully aware of the answers to each of these questions and is asking them to verify whether the student has, in fact, read the book and grasps its fundamentals. The instructor might expand and shift to curious open questions at some point.

What was your favorite part of the book?

Who was the character you connected with the most?

What do you think was the moral or message of the book?

Another place where leading open questions are used frequently is in the court system. In any courtroom scene where a lawyer is examining a witness, you will most likely observe the lawyer asking leading open questions, questions he or she already knows the answer to and whose purpose is to allow the witness to tell his or her story in a way that the lawyer thinks will provide the necessary information to the judge and jury.

Examples:

What did you notice when you arrived at the scene?

Who else was at the scene?

What did you do after you arrived at the scene?

What did you do next?

Value of Leading Open Questions: Leading open questions do just that: lead the responder to a specific conclusion or end point. They narrow the available options, and verify an answer already known by the person asking the question. They can confirm what has occurred already. Knowledge can be tested, which can result in a "right or wrong" answer where the responder may be seeking approval from the asker. Outcomes may be judging or blaming.

Judging Open Questions

Sometimes we think we are asking a curious open question because we don't know the answer, and we start the question with how, who, what, where, when, or why. However, when the question contains negative words that convey judging, blaming, and shaming, we are asking a judging open question. This approach results in pushing the responder's emotional buttons, triggering an outcome that does not generate curiosity or learning.

Parent: How could you be so clumsy and spill your milk? What is going on with you?

Although the parent may not know how the milk was spilled, the manner in which the question has been asked implies they do. The child might hear, "I am clumsy. I can't get this right," which results in them feeling judged, blamed, and perhaps shamed. Instead of creating a moment of learning, the question may cause the child to shut down or become really angry. Introducing these negative emotions into the conversation compromises the opportunity for learning and may result in the child feeling more miserable than they already do about spilling their milk and making a mess. How could you change this question to make it a curious and open one?

> **Parent** (ensuring tone and facial expressions are neutral and non-blaming): Oops, looks like milk got spilled. What happened here?

Going back to your listening skills, how could your nonverbal communication cues compromise the curious and open conversation you want to create?

We have found parents and leaders in many situations tend to revert to judging open questions either through the words used or nonverbal cues messaged. Typically in these situations, something has gone wrong, and they are looking to cast blame somewhere. Casting blame removes any opportunity for reflection and learning, so the person being addressed feels even worse than he or she already did, if in fact he or she has made a mistake. Changing the conversational strategy to asking curious open questions allows the leader or parent to discover what really went on and enables everyone to participate in finding a solution, one that creates learning and minimizes the possibility of the same event reoccurring.

> **Leader**: I just realized the account information that was to be on my desk this morning is not here. How could you mess this up? I don't have the information I asked for.
>
> **Manager**: I am sorry. I won't let this happen again.
>
> **Leader**: You had better not if you want to keep your job.

Here is what happens when the leader is less judging:

Leader: I just realized the account information that was to be on my desk this morning is not here. Why is the information not here?

Manager: I am sorry. I forgot you needed it this early.

Leader: You are usually prompt with my requests, so I will let it pass this time.

However, in both these situations, the leader is still judging to a degree, and the conversation does not lead to the disclosure of what is going on or how things can be changed so this situation does not arise again, meaning there is no opportunity for learning.

Here is what can happen when the leader shifts from a judging open question to a curious open question.

Leader: I just realized the account information that was to be on my desk this morning is not here. I find you are usually on top of such things, so I am wondering what happened today?

Manager: I am sorry. I was not able to get the data from the others until a few minutes ago, and I am just now completing the information, so you should have it in about thirty minutes.

Leader: What was the reason for getting the data just now?

Manager: I sent out my request yesterday, and no one realized I needed the information as quickly as I did.

Leader: How could you change this when making a request in the future?

Manager: I think I will add both my deadline and when I need the information from them. I think they will better appreciate my needs this way and provide it to me in a timely manner.

Leader: Great—it sounds as if you have a figured out a solution that will work for you and ensure you have information to me in a timely way. Thank you.

Of the examples, which of these do you prefer? What are your reasons for this choice? We have found when working with groups using this non-blaming approach, more often than not, there are several reasons for the error, not just the one that seems to be most apparent. When curiosity is brought into this conversation, an opportunity to explore causes and solutions can result in learning such that the same issue does not reoccur.

Value of Judging Open Questions: We cannot see any value in these questions. They promote blaming and shaming, which does not help us to see, hear, and understand others or to build relationships. Being aware of the power of these questions can help us avoid them at all times.

Let's take a look at what each type of question might look like in a single situation:

A friend is going for a job interview, and she really wants this office job. She feels she has the skills and experience required, and the job could be a good fit and a great opportunity for her. She has talked to you about what she might wear; she has a new low-cut red dress that she bought for a party and is thinking of wearing it.

Closed question: Do you want to wear your low-cut red dress for this interview?

Judging closed question: Do you *really* want to wear your low-cut red dress to your interview?

Curious open question: What is your reason for wearing your low-cut red dress to your interview?

Leading open question: How appropriate is your low-cut red dress for this interview?

Judging open question: Why would you want to wear such a low-cut dress to your interview?

Building Relationships through Curious Open Questions

We recently heard a fable that asked what a person is comprised of. The response was that a person is made up of two equal parts, one positive and one negative. How we show up depends on which part we feed more. We liked this fable because it demonstrates that using a positive, less critical strategy toward ourselves and others feeds the positive self. In turn, this supports our curiosity and allows us to build effective relationships in which we seek to understand others.

I (Kathy) have learned over the years that when I am critical of others, even in my head, I feel somewhat "icky." I can't think of any other way to describe this feeling. I find if I really focus on positive thoughts about me and others, I can suspend my need for control, thus allowing for ambiguity, and create the space in a conversation where I can not only hear others, but learn from them. I feel I am seeing, hearing, and understanding them, and as I begin to convey this through my open questions, I can sense they are also seeing, hearing, and understanding me. I love being in this space. It is energetic and yet peaceful, nourishing, and fun. I find I can connect with others when I allow myself to suspend judgment of myself and others, and am open and thus accepting of everyone (including me) for who they are.

I (Kirsten) have found that women tend to be especially critical of other women, which is so surprising and sad to me. I noticed it most just after I had my kids, the time when I thought women were supposed to ban together and unite! I saw judgment of breastfeeding vs. bottle feeding, stay at home mom vs. working mom, organic food vs. non-organic food, public school vs. private school—the list was endless, and each side more convinced they were right than the next, leaving a wake of shame, failure, and self-doubt.

In a world where women are still not earning as much as men or receiving the same opportunities, where we are expected to "do it all" while looking like a supermodel from a glossy magazine, it is so sad to me that women aren't more supportive and understanding of each other, redefining what is "successful." My hope is that when women become more curious with each other, and more understanding of themselves and others (without judgment), our cultural conversation will shift. It is not only important for ourselves; it is important for our daughters. We are starting to see this shift happen, and we encourage you to think about how you show up for your community—both personally and professionally. What are you feeding in yourself and others?

Looking at all five types of questions, we can see that three of them serve the purpose of building relationships in conversation. The closed question can be used to confirm paraphrasing or to check for accuracy. The leading open question can be used to better understand someone's comprehension of an issue, clarify a story, or confirm details. The curious open question, our personal favorite, can be used to create possibility, better understand each other, and develop innovation.

How Curious Open Questions Support Strong Leadership

In many situations, people struggle with asking curious open questions because they need to achieve a specific outcome from a conversation. In our experience, leaders (or parents) find it challenging to understand how they can be curious when they need someone to change a behavior or a specific outcome in order to feel successful. Here are some specific ways asking curious open questions can support strong leadership and result in a positive outcome for all involved parties.

Curious Open Questions Support Needed Context

Imagine you are a leader who is told you must ensure employees are not absent from work more than five days in any given year. As the leader, you are uncomfortable about having these conversations with employees. You are concerned you will be seen as the enemy and want to maintain the trust and respect of your employees. You have asked an employee (Christian) to come to your office for a meeting to discuss this new organization-wide policy.

Leader: Hi, Christian. As you may know, our organization has noticed a high level of absence throughout. Based on industry norms, we have determined that we will work to meet a goal of five days of total absence in any given year. All leaders are having conversations with employees who report to them, advising them of this new policy. I notice you have been absent from work for twenty-five days over the past twelve months. This is higher than the new standard set by the organization. What can you do to ensure you are at work for more days this coming year?

Christian: Well, I am not sure. I think I had a cold that would not go away, and my son was sick, which meant I was up half the night, and then I was too tired to come to work. I can't remember what else happened.

Leader: It sounds as if your life is challenging at times with a young son. What strategy can you put in place to try to minimize the number of days you are absent this year?

Christian: I don't know. I can't tell when I am getting a cold until I have one, and similarly, I can't predict when my son is going to get sick. I suppose I could try to take better care of myself, get a flu shot, and get plenty of rest so I am less susceptible to colds. I am not sure what I can do about my son because he is in daycare, and even though they have a policy that says only kids who are well should be there, lots of kids are dropped off when they are sick and should not be there.

Leader: I think taking better care of yourself is a good idea. It sounds as if you respect the policy around illness at your daycare. What might you be prepared to do to support the daycare in upholding their policy around sick kids?

Christian: I could talk to them because I do find this frustrating. I stay home to look after my son when he is sick, and others don't respect the policy in the same way. I am prepared to talk to them and explain how allowing sick kids to be there puts the kids who are well at risk.

Leader: Christian, it sounds as if you have a plan. I really respect the work you do and the contribution you make to the department. It sounds as if you are prepared to work to ensure you support the organization moving forward. Perhaps we could connect in three months, and see how things are going.

Christian: Okay. In the meantime, I will do what I can to minimize my sick leave.

We have found that once our clients understood they could start the conversation by establishing context, they no longer felt they were the "bad guy," as they could focus on the company policy. Rather than personally holding the employees accountable, they were able to hold them accountable to non-negotiable policies outlined by the company. As a result, they became more comfortable and able to stay in a curious place from which they could support the employee in developing a plan that could work for them. There was no "you versus me," as they were in it together.

Curious Open Questions Support Effective Telling

We have mentioned various times how telling is passé, from an era we are leaving behind. And yet we all know that sometimes telling is the best response one can give to support another person. Like most things, telling has an appropriate time and place. We think the time and place for telling is in response to a question, typically a curious open question, in which the content of the question includes a request for help, support, or ideas. In such a situation, you have an opportunity to respond by telling the person what you think will work for them, providing the advice requested. That is the key: "requested." When we are asked for our advice, we already know that the person is open to listening to what we have to say because otherwise she wouldn't have asked. She will be attentive and open to the advice suggested. Most of us are eager to tell and provide advice when it is not requested. In a situation when advice is requested, the teller will feel respected and honored, as they can see the asker wants them to share their wisdom, their knowledge, and experience.

Curious Open Questions Help Leaders Hold Focus

Maybe you are a leader chairing a meeting with your team or working with one or more employees. Or you are a parent, and you need to have a conversation with a young child or teenager. Or maybe you are a professional person to whom a client or patient has come for counsel. In all these cases, the thought of asking curious open questions may seem inappropriate because you will appear lacking in knowledge or control. Shifting to a place of total ambiguity may not work. You are not feeling comfortable with this approach. This is perfectly natural. We suggest that before you start a meeting with your team, child, or patient, you intentionally determine your desired outcome, and then hold the focus in order to keep moving toward that place during the conversation. Asking curious open questions that create space will help generate new ideas to achieve your outcome.

> **Leader chairing a meeting:** I provided all of you with a copy of the new directive from head office. There is an expectation that we will find a way to embrace this directive within the next sixty days. How do you see us achieving this?

The directive is process related; the leader sets the context, and the curious open question creates the focus. The conversation is now open to all participants as they come up with ideas, piggyback off the ideas of others, and collaborate towards a solution. If comments begin to drift away from the focus (such as "I can't believe they have asked us to do this," or "This is so unreasonable, and we should not have to do it"), it is the responsibility of the leader to once again ask a curious open question. This will take the participants back to the topic at hand and hold the focus for the group.

The parent having the following conversation with her child about an incident at school can set a goal to better understand what happened without casting blame.

Parent: Stella, I received a call from the school today and learned that Parker was quite upset because of what went on at the playground during recess. I understand you were there. What caused Parker to become so upset?

Stella: Oh, he always gets so upset at nothing. He is such a baby.

Parent: Well, Stella, I would like to know what went on and need you to describe to me what happened.

Once again, the parent is holding the focus and not deviating, even when the child attempts to create a diversion.

Perhaps you have heard someone say, "That was such a great question," and you have wondered what that meant. How often do you feel you have been asked a great question or have asked such a question? How do you know when such a question has been posed? For most people being asked such a question, they will say they know a question is great when it causes them to pause, reflect, and reconsider, which usually leads to an "aha" moment—a moment they learn something new, something they may not have thought of before. This experience creates great energy and enthusiasm, allowing others to piggyback off the revelation and build ideas that generate greater curiosity on the parts of all involved, leading to new opportunities and further innovation. That is the value and richness of asking questions!

You too can create great questions, ones that will generate curiosity, reflection, and learning for everyone concerned. We invite you to set an intention to ask curious open questions. How many curious open questions will you ask today?

How the Five Listening Choices
Determine the Questions We Ask

As a reminder, here are the five Listening Choices we always have available to us, as well as their characteristics and their practical uses. We have now added a column to this chart that lists the types of questions that support each choice of listening.

Our Listening Choices	What Listener Is Thinking	Characteristics	Uses	Type of Questions That Support Listening Choice
Choice 1: Ignore the speaker	Listener ignores what is being said	Does not listen Is closed to all ideas Is silent Not interested in understanding others Focused elsewhere	When listener wants silence When all else has failed when trying to end a conversation When listener does not value building connection When listener desires to shut someone down	Not asking questions

Choice 2: **Focus on Me**	"If I were you, I wouldn't do that." "I want you to . . . ." "I think you should . . . ." "I can't believe you would . . . ."	Listens to pay attention Is closed to ideas of others Judges self Judges others and compares to self Needs to be right or fears being wrong Does not attempt to understand others	When listener wants to share own perspective As a response to the question, "What would you do?" In mentoring and professional advising contexts When hanging out with friends or family In emergency situations	Closed questions Judging closed questions Leading open questions Judging open questions
Choice 3: **Focus on You**	"You should . . . ." "You need to . . . ." "You have to . . . ."	Listens to pay attention Is closed to ideas of others Judges self and others Desires/needs to help (even if no request for help was made) Does not attempt to understand others Offers an expert opinion	When providing advice When providing information, particularly as a professional such as a doctor, lawyer, mentor, or counselor	Closed questions Judging closed questions Leading open questions Judging open questions

Choice 4: **Focus on** **Understanding**	"How did you do that?" "What would you do?"	Actively listens Is curious Seeks to understand others Does not judge Tests assumptions Allows for ambiguity Demonstrates empathy	When desiring to understand perspectives of others When gaining information When supporting learning In coaching, mentoring, and professional advising contexts	Curious open questions Closed questions
Choice 5: **Focus on Us**	"I need you to . . . ." "How do you think we can achieve this?" "We need to . . . ." "What can I do to help you achieve this?"	Actively listens Is curious Describes own interest Is open to perspectives of others Seeks to understand others Creates common ground to move forward Demonstrates empathy Remains invested in the outcome	In negotiation In conflict resolution When collaborating as teams, leaders, parents, etc. When developing goals When supporting others	Curious open questions Leading open questions Closed questions

Clearly, how we choose to listen will influence the types of questions we ask. For example, if we are listening using Choice 2 (Focus on Me), we will most likely respond with a telling comment or a closed question so we can narrow the options or advise. If we listen using Choice 4 (Focus on Understanding), then our response will likely be open and curious, with no attachment to the outcome; however, after listening to what is said, we may decide the connection will be best served by responding with telling or a closed question. It is most common for people to listen in Choice 2 (Focus on Me) and 3 (Focus on You); therefore most people respond as tellers rather than asking any questions at all because telling is a natural byproduct of these listening choices. Whatever choice of listening you initially make, intentionally asking curious open questions will help you shift to Choice 4 and 5 listening.

We all come into this world naturally curious. As adults, we just need to be reminded of what we already know. You have now re-learned your Curiosity Skills, skills that can support you in creating the relationships in which you can understand others and they can understand you. Now it's time to get curious about yourself. In Part Two, we will share strategies that will help you better understand yourself through curiosity, so that you'll be better equipped to understand others.

Take Action

1. Looking back at the types of questions discussed in this chapter, what types of questions do you find yourself using most? How come?

2. How does that type of question support you in understanding others?

3. Looking forward, what type of question will you practice using in conversation? How come?

4. How can you use the five Listening Choices to support you in your curiosity and understanding others?

Part Two

USING CURIOSITY TO UNDERSTAND YOURSELF

CHAPTER 5

DEFINE YOUR VALUES

*It's not hard to make decisions
when you know what your values are.*
Roy Disney

Values clear
& identified

Many years ago, when Kirsten was little, a friend and neighbor arrived home from work just as I (Kathy) was walking her and her brother across the street. He seemed miffed and proceeded to tell me how a friend of mine had kept him waiting for forty-five minutes that morning. He then said, "Being late is the most selfish thing anyone can do."

It stopped me in my tracks. I couldn't help but think of the many times I had been late to meet someone, or just not as aware of being on time as I could have been. I had never thought that maybe, just maybe, the person I was meeting would be upset if I were late. It didn't bother me if people were a little late to meet me, and I had never considered others might not feel the same way.

Understanding Individual Values

We all have an individual set of values, those non-negotiable characteristics that make us who we are. These values define our being, our core, how we show up in life. When we live aligned with our values, we feel congruent, experiencing less resistance and conflict as we move through life. We feel connected to our self. We feel happy and successful, according to our individual definitions of happiness and success. When we are not living in alignment with our values, we may feel slightly disconnected, and life can seem like a struggle. For example, if family is your top value and you are working seventy hours a week, you will most likely feel internal stress and conflict, as you are not able to spend as much time with your family as you want to.

When you understand your values, you can refer to them to help you make decisions about how you want to live your life. You'll have greater self-awareness, stronger/authentic relationships, greater integrity, and more credibility as a leader. You'll create more opportunities for consistent behavior, which will also help you be a better parent, son/daughter, partner, and friend. And you'll be able to make choices that lead you to your own happiness and success and to build authentic relationships.

> *I stopped living according to my core values. I knew what*
> *I was doing was wrong but thought only about myself and*
> *thought I could get away with whatever I wanted to do.*
> **Tiger Woods**

Although we tend to define conflict as angry or emotional exchanges with others, conflict actually begins long before that negative exchange, at the level of our values. When our values conflict with or are not respected by others, our emotional buttons get touched or even pushed really hard. We feel ignored, offended, and/or disrespected, which is exactly what happened that morning years ago with my friend and neighbor. His value of time was disrespected, and it pushed his emotional buttons, hard. So hard that his late morning meeting still upset him at the end of his workday in the early evening. How do you think that influenced his relationship with my friend?

Take a moment and think of a situation when you were offended by the action of another person, and perhaps no one else found the action to be offensive. What was it about that action that caused you to feel indignant? Identifying actions that you find offensive can help you identify your personal values and make sense of your emotional buttons.

While it was important to my neighbor to be on time, it was apparent that my friend did not value a commitment to time in the same way he did. Their values were different, and so being on time for a meeting was not that important to my friend. Although my neighbor felt disrespected, my friend probably had no idea he had offended a colleague to that extent.

Through this experience I learned that just because punctuality was not overly important to me, it was to others, and I decided I would respect that in others and commit to being on time. For the most part, I have been able to honor that commitment, and when for some reason I can't, I always have my cell phone at the ready to call and give the person I am meeting a "heads up" with an ETA.

Identifying Your Values

Over the years, we have learned that very few people take the time to understand their values. Nevertheless, your values are there whether you choose to identify them or not. And discovering your core values can be fun!

Here is a list of values we have created for you to explore with curiosity so you can discover what your values are and what they represent to you. Which of the following words reflect your core values?

Accountability	Equality	Justice
Accomplishment	Excellence	Knowledge
Achievement	Family	Leadership
Adventure	Fairness	Learning
Arts	Freedom	Listening
Authority	Friendship	Living my passion
Authenticity	Fun	Loyalty
Challenge	Gratitude	Love
Change	Honor	Money
Commitment	Hard work	Passion
Community	Harmony	Peace
Connection	Health	Pleasure
Cooperation	Honesty	Positive attitude
Creativity	Helping others	Power
Curiosity	Inner peace, calm	Privacy
Discovery	Innovation	Public service
Empathy	Integrity	Relationships

Respect for self and others	Simplicity	Transparency
Responsibility	Spirituality	Tolerance
Unity	Stability	Trust
Punctuality	Status	Truth
Safety	Success	Understanding
Satisfying others	Teamwork	Unity
Security	Time management	Wisdom
Service of others	Tradition	
	Tranquility	

If the words on our list don't connect with you, Google the term "values" to find more words that may resonate for you. Once you have a list of values to consider, take the time to get curious, review the list, reflect, and underline all the words that resonate with you. Look for words that you are drawn to, with which you feel a connection, a meaning. Then, narrow down your list of values to the top three that best resonate with who you are and how you want to live your life. These top three core values are the radar, or compass, that consciously or unconsciously guides your decision-making process and shows you whether you are living authentically or not.

My top three core values are:

1.

2.

3.

Now, take the time to define exactly what each of these values means to you. The definition you give a value is yours and only yours. For example, two people may value adventure, but while one may define adventure as doing something new and different, another may define it as taking extreme risks, like jumping out of a plane as a skydiver. Don't worry about how other people define these terms. How do *you* define them?

As you look at your top three values and their definitions, ask yourself:

1. How do these values make me feel good about myself?
2. How do I feel when these values aren't present in my life?
3. How do I feel when they are present in my life?
4. How do these values represent things I would support, even if my choice isn't popular and puts me in the minority?

If you have trouble answering the four questions above, then stay curious (in other words, be present, listen to your thoughts, dig deeper, and ask yourself curious open questions), and keep playing with your list until you get the top three that "click." Over the next few days and weeks, keep revisiting your values to ensure that they are authentic and representative of you. Remember, there are no right or wrong answers. Your core value list is for you and you only.

As you create your list, it is important to remember that this exercise is not about identifying the values you think you might like to have; it is about the values you actually have today. If you don't take the time to discover your real, true values, those qualities that make you who you are, you will never be in alignment (because you cannot be in full alignment with values that are not your own), nor will you develop greater self-awareness and the ability to truly understand yourself.

Living Your Values

Once you have identified and defined your values, you will begin to notice when you are living them—and when you're not. When you're living your values, you will feel really good about what is going on in your life. Many describe this feeling as being grounded, at peace, or steady. When you're not, you may feel irritable, conflicted, or lost.

Looking at your list, on a scale of 1 to 10, how fully do you live each one of your values in your life? A more visual way to answer this question is to think of a paint-by-number picture with just three colors and ten areas that can be painted with each color, so you have a total of thirty areas to paint. Each color represents one of your values. For each number selected on your scale, you can paint one section, so if you have a value of honesty and rate it a 9, you can paint 9 of the sections in the color you assign to honesty.

After you have repeated this activity with each of the three colors, consider how complete your picture is. How fully are you living your values? Is your picture vibrant, filled with the three colors evenly distributed, or spotty with little color, creating a bland canvas? How can you make your picture more vibrant and alive? What do you need to do to create the fulfilling life you want, one in which your values are aligned with your actions?

If you find you are not living fully, how can you bring more life to the values (colors) that appear to be neglected? Reflect back on the definitions you created for each value. What would your life be like if each one of these was a 10, so that you were fully living your life? How would you feel living your life this way?

Take a minute and visualize what your life would be like, how you would show up for yourself and with others.

What would be different in your life?

What is in your life now that you can build on?

What is getting in your way, stopping you from living your life fully and aligning your values with your actions and your intentions?

For most of us, life holds more than just one dimension. Along with a personal life, we may have a professional life, a family life, and a social life. If we want to live with congruence, aligning our values in all aspects of our lives is important. Looking at your three core values, how do they show up in your personal life? How do they show up in your family life, your professional/work life with colleagues, and your social life with friends? What would your paint-by-number picture look like from the perspective of each of the four dimensions below?

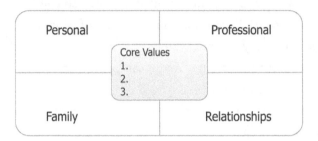

If you find you are not in alignment, or as aligned as you would like to be, use the chart below to see how you can realign your life to reflect your core values.

Core Value 1:

	How are you currently honoring your core value?	What are you noticing?	What can you do to bring yourself closer to alignment?
Personal			
Professional			
Family			
Social			

Core Value 2:

	How are you currently honoring your core value?	What are you noticing?	What can you do to bring yourself closer to alignment?
Personal			
Professional			
Family			
Social			

Core Value 3:

	How are you currently honoring your core value?	What are you noticing?	What can you do to bring yourself closer to alignment?
Personal			
Professional			
Family			
Social			

Looking at your relationships personally and professionally, what are some ways that you can honor and respect the values of others, even if they are not the same as yours? How can you use curiosity to support those relationships?

Understanding Group Values

Imagine you own a company, and you are leading the sales team. Your personal core values are honesty, responsibility, and accountability. In order to meet your monthly numbers, everyone on the team needs to make their sales quota. You notice that the sales aren't coming in, and you know you aren't going to meet your targeted numbers. At the end of the day, it is your responsibility to make sure that the sales are made; it is your company, and you are responsible for making sure your team gets paid.

You begin to notice some of your team members are gossiping, some are taking long coffee breaks, and others are just avoiding each other. You're frustrated, because you need work to get done. You meet with your team to see how you can finalize sales and meet your numbers. One team member says she is overwhelmed. She is doing the best she can and is getting the work done when she can do it. Her child has been sick, and she needs to focus on her child's recovery. Another says he has called all his "A clients" and should not be expected to make cold calls. He has an established book of clients that he has collected over his many years of service, and his focus is on enhancing those relationships, not creating new ones. Another says that she has called everyone, but no one is calling her back, so she is just waiting.

Frustrated and dissatisfied, you do some investigating on your own and reach out to your clients, only to learn that all of your team members aren't getting your clients the necessary information and aren't following up the way they said they were. You learn that clients are either passing or going with someone else. Infuriated, you think, *How can my team do this to me?* You feel they have lied to you; they aren't completing the responsibilities of their job, and you are now accountable for their actions. You take over every account and start doing the work yourself because you know you will get it done and need to lock in these sales. Meanwhile, your team is frustrated with you because they feel you are being unrealistic and expecting them to do too much. As far as they are concerned, they are doing their job, and now you are telling them it isn't good enough. At the end of the day, no one is working together as a team, no one's needs are being met (including the company's), and no one is happy about it.

This kind of scenario happens all the time, both in the workplace and in the home. When a group of people connects as a team, a family, or a community, they each bring their unique values to that group, creating a much larger set of values. In the story above, the values of the owner/leader are coming through loud and clear at the expense of everyone else on the team. She is holding everyone to her set of personal values, even though the team is not aware of what those values are. As we just saw, imposing one's personal values on a group without discussion can result in frustration for everyone, especially if the group is to spend a great deal of time together. Relationships can be tested, with outcomes that are not always optimal. Creating group values can help a group define itself as a collective unit able to function together, rather than just a group of competing individuals. It provides a valuable joint compass that helps them navigate challenges together. It also sets clear expectations for those in the group or organization to which they can be held accountable.

This team's lack of clarity about their group values almost cost the owner her company. But once the team set clear values for the group, the team members understood what their expectations were and what they were to value. They could figure out how their personal core values fit with the team values. Now, as a group, they all shared the same focus. Setting clear values also allowed the owner of the company to hold her team members accountable to the values they identified and agreed upon, rather than having the accountability fall solely on her. As issues came up, defaulting to the group values as the compass for accountability provided consistency. Engagement in work became easier for everyone.

The same is true for a family. Defining and developing a set of values for a family provides a joint compass that helps them navigate life together with clarity and focus. In fact, the same is true for any group of people. I (Kathy) once had a conversation with someone who claimed to have worked with one of the drug cartels. He spoke with pride about the values of his cartel, which included trust, honor, and hard work. Although his definitions of those values may have been different than mine or yours, each member of that group knew the meaning of those values and lived by them.

Of course, every group already has a set of values the collective uses to function together, whether they know it or not. For some, interrupting each other during a meeting may be the way they create innovative solutions (perhaps called "brainstorming"). For another group, interrupting each other may be seen as disrespectful and disruptive of their creative process.

For some, ethical practices may be a non-negotiable value. Others may value money more than ethics; therefore it's okay to cross ethical lines if a big payday results. How do you think someone with a value of ethical integrity would feel working in an organization where acquiring money at any cost is the primary value? What will happen to that person if he or she stays in that environment?

A team or group of any kind can get curious and create their own list of values to define what they respect and what is important to them. We invite you to get curious about the values of your own groups and relationships, and use the chart below to identify them. Once defined, these values will help to bind your group together, clarifying what makes it unique and special.

Group Values

Group	Value	What does it mean?	How do you honor and respect it?

Obstacles to Living Your Values

Beliefs

Human beings have conversational blind spots. These are beliefs
that get in the way of us connecting mind to mind with others, and
where we have blind spots, we also have conflict and breakdowns.
Judith Glaser, *Conversational Intelligence*

Some people consider values and beliefs to be the same. We do not. We see a belief as something we accept as a truth that arises from our life experiences, our family of origin, our teachers, and others who have influenced our lives. A belief may not be true, while our values are our non-negotiable truths that anchor each of us in our lives.

There are two types of beliefs: objective and subjective. An objective belief is one we accept as truth based on the evidence created by others. For example, we all know the earth is round, although most of us have never been out in space to confirm this belief. We just believe it to be so. A subjective belief is one based on our own experience and the "truth" that arises from this experience.

The challenge with beliefs is that many of them no longer serve us in any way. They can create blocks that prevent us from living in alignment with our values and doing things we might enjoy and be good at now. They can also create a blind spot that leads us to judge ourselves or others, which can create limitations for us.

I (Kirsten) once had a client who was a talented graphic artist but did not believe in her own talent, which resulted in her struggling in all aspects of her life. We used to meet outside her studio. She had set up an outdoor living space behind her office with a sofa leaning up against a wall that had been painted by different artists. As soon as she sat in the sofa, she would turn her body towards me in such a way as to breathe in the art on the wall. It was clear that it grounded her. I started to get curious with her, trying to understand how she came to be a graphic artist. As she started to tell me about her journey, she blurted out, "Well, it isn't a real job anyway, so what does it matter?"

"As a person who makes a living as a graphic artist, it sounds like it would matter to you. How come you say that?" I asked her.

"Everyone knows that."

"Who is everyone?" I wondered.

She was now visibly frustrated. "My parents have been saying it my whole life, telling me to get a 'real' job because drawing isn't real work," she snapped.

"Okay, so what do they consider to be 'real' work?" Now my curiosity was peaked.

"Doctors, lawyers, teachers—you know, people who have value." And then she started to cry.

There it was, unraveling before us. The reason behind her struggle was so close and yet so difficult for her to see. Her parents' belief that drawing wasn't real work became her belief, and she believed that since she wasn't doing "real" work, she didn't have any value. The problem was that she was incredibly talented, and the beliefs she adopted from her parents were blinding her to her reality. While she may not have had faith in her abilities as an artist, she valued the craft. She had tremendous respect and value for her peers who did the same work. In other words, this belief clearly conflicted with her values.

In her head, she knew it was crazy to let her parents' beliefs, beliefs that she didn't even share, hold her back. However, in her heart, it was impossible to just let them go. It was easier for her to continue to believe she was no good and had no value. Unfortunately, the belief messaged by her parents was not just holding her back, it was sabotaging her life— and she had been completely blind to it!

Reframing

When beliefs no longer support the way you want to live your life, reframing is an effective strategy to explore such beliefs and position them so they are no longer blind spots creating inertia. Reframing allows one to take a situation, experience, perspective, or belief and use curious open questions to look at it differently, opening up an opportunity to create a new or different outcome. Some curious open questions that support reframing are: How can I look at this differently? What have I learned? How can I leverage this experience? How is this supporting me? What am I missing? How can I explore this in a new way?

Once our graphic artist client understood what was holding her back and that the beliefs standing in her way were not actually her own, she was able to slowly let go of them. Each time she found herself self-sabotaging and letting her old beliefs resurface, she would stop herself and use curiosity to reframe her negative perspective into a positive one, which would change her experience. So her old belief that her work held no value, and therefore she was no good, became, "I value art, and I value artists; therefore as an artist I have value and am capable of real work. Artists create beauty and have talent not everyone has. I value beautiful things and am fortunate to be an artist who has talent."

As she explored the different ways being an artist held meaning for her, it became easier for her to recognize what triggered her self-sabotaging beliefs. When someone complimented her, instead of immediately thinking, "Yeah, but . . . ," she was able to recognize the sabotaging trigger, use curiosity to reframe that self-sabotaging belief, acknowledge her talent, and accept the compliment with grace.

We invite you to think of a belief that may no longer be serving you. Perhaps as a child you were told you were not able to do something such as sing a song, draw a picture, take a photograph, or play a sport. This statement may have become your own belief, and it has resulted in your avoiding the activity or has otherwise influenced choices you have made. Next, test your belief through curious open questions: "What makes me think this belief is true? How is this belief supporting my values? Where did this belief come from?" Keep asking curious open questions until you feel you have made sense of your belief, where it came from, the role it plays in your life, and how it is supporting you (or not). Then, reframe your belief by asking curious open questions with the intention to flip the belief around and look at it with a new perspective. Ask yourself questions like, "How can I look at this situation differently so it supports my values? What would happen if I choose to let go of this belief? How can I turn this belief holding me back into learning that will propel me forward? What assumptions am I making about this belief that are holding me back?" (We will talk more about assumptions in the next section.)

Exploring new ways to understand our beliefs, the roles they play in our lives, and the influence beliefs have on us allows us to better understand ourselves, our choices, how we build relationships, and how we align with our values. As we challenge our beliefs, or discover new ways of seeing them through reframing, we can determine what we want to do with our beliefs. If we decide the belief still serves us, we can embrace it, and if we determine it no longer serves us and is creating a blind spot for us, we can let it go in order to embrace the life we want. When it comes to beliefs, the choice is always ours.

Assumptions

An assumption is anything we take for granted, whether or not it is true. Our society is built on assumptions. We all know the expressions "assumptions make an ass of you and me" and "never assume anything," yet we still regularly make assumptions.

Sometimes our beliefs lead us to make assumptions. Imagine you see a young man dressed casually, standing beside a really expensive car. If you had the belief that wealthy people drive expensive cars, your assumption might be, *This kid is really wealthy.* But if the person walking next to you had the belief that hard work affords you the money to buy expensive things, he might assume, *This kid is a really hard worker.* Of course, neither may actually be true about this young man.

Assumptions can pose a major obstacle to living out our values because taking things for granted sometimes interferes with our ability to discern our truth or what our reality truly is.

So our client who was a graphic artist assumed that everyone shared the belief that graphic artists didn't do real work, which conflicted with her ability to align with her core value. In reality, the belief was her parents', not hers, and her assumption that everyone shared her parents' belief was not true. Understanding where the belief came from and that her assumption wasn't true allowed her to let go of both her parents' belief and her assumption, so she could live in alignment with her core values.

Not all assumptions are connected to our values and beliefs. We take things for granted in every corner of our lives. But if we choose to be curious, we can test our assumptions when we recognize them and learn from them.

I (Kirsten) have made many assumptions in my life and haven't always learned from them. But here is a wonderful example of how one of my assumptions made an ass of me, and I learned never to do it again.

Early one morning, my son, who was three at the time, was supposed to be getting ready for preschool. It was a busy day, and I had one foot out the door when I noticed he had no pants on. I asked him about it, and he said he wanted his pants from yesterday. I told him those pants were dirty, and I asked him to pick a clean pair of pants so we could go.

"No!" he said, raising his voice and getting visibly upset, "I want my pants from yesterday!"

Trying to keep my cool, thinking I was doing all the "right" things, I got down to his level, looked him in the eye, and calmly said, "I heard you; you want your pants from yesterday. I feel like you aren't hearing me. I told you they are really dirty. Please pick a clean pair of pants so that we can go."

This was not the answer he was hoping for. Frustrated, he stomped his foot, looked me square in the eye, and screamed, "NO! I WANT my pants from yesterday. I want them. I WANT them!"

He started crying and became really upset. I was getting angry, frustrated, and annoyed. I was late. He wasn't listening to me. It wasn't even 8 a.m., and I was already feeling exhausted.

I admit this was not my proudest parenting moment. Wanting this to end and get out the door as quickly as possible, I turned on my heel, got the dirty pants, and shoved them his way, saying, "Fine. Wear your dirty pants. Put them on now; we need to go."

Through snotty tears, my son took the pants, reached into the pocket, and pulled out a toy. Then he proceeded to put on a clean pair of pants, wipes his nose, and said, "Let's go."

Dumbfounded, I looked at him and said, "Oh, you *wanted* your pants. You didn't want to wear your pants. You just wanted them for your toy."

I wanted the world to swallow me whole. My son was being really clear that he wanted his pants. I was making the assumption that he wanted his pants in order to wear them, and as I was so focused on my own needs, I wasn't being curious or asking questions as to why he so desperately wanted his pants.

I could see the hurt in his eyes, and I quickly tried to make a repair and apologize to my son. When I asked him what I could do differently next time so this wouldn't happen again, he looked at me and quietly said, "Mom, you could have just asked me."

He was right. If I had just asked, we would have gotten out the door more quickly, without the emotional drama and strain on our relationship. I was completely schooled by my son. At three years old, he understood the power of curiosity.

One thing we have learned over the years is that it does not matter what we assume to be a reality; we are rarely correct. When we take the time to test our assumptions, we always learn something that reshapes our thoughts and even our beliefs in a way that helps us become curious and learn. Once you start listening for assumptions, you will find that they're everywhere; you'll hear them in most conversations. If your friend mentions casually, "We had such a good time at the party the other night," you may assume that your friend's definition of a good time is the same as yours, so you immediately conjure up a picture in your head of people dancing, chatting, and having drinks. But you can test your assumption simply by asking an open question such as, "What made it such a good time for you?"

Although beliefs and assumptions may pose obstacles to living our values, reframing and testing them can create great learning and lead to greater understanding. Using our Curiosity Skills to become present to actively listen, making a listening choice, and asking curious open questions helps us understand what others are saying. In this way, we no longer take anything for granted; we gain clarity and become open to new and different thoughts, experiences, or ideas.

Now that we have defined our values, in the next chapter we will identify our wants that align with our values and learn to instill boundaries to protect both.

Take Action

1. Use the charts in this chapter to explore and identify your values, define what they mean, and decide how you want to honor your values in your life. Be sure to explore both your individual and group values in all areas of your life—personal, professional, family, and social—and see how your values align in all the aspects of your life.

2. As you explore your values, make sure you are aware of the obstacles that can challenge them, such as your beliefs and assumptions. Pay attention to:

   a. *Beliefs*: Any time something follows a "yeah, but . . ." in your mind, you are most likely encountering a belief. We invite you to listen for this phrase, and when you encounter it, use your Curiosity Skills to identify this belief, understand it better, and discover how it is serving you in living your core values.

   b. *Assumptions*: Assumptions can be so much fun to test. We make them based our values and our beliefs, and they occur in every conversation, guaranteed. Explore the assumptions you are making in your life. Then, anytime you notice someone making a general statement, instead of taking it for granted, ask curious open questions to help you to better understand what is meant.

   c. *Reframing*: As you explore your beliefs and assumptions, use your Curiosity Skills to reframe and look at each one with a different lens. Use curious open questions as you reframe, such as, "How do I know this to be true? What am I missing? How can I look at this differently?"

CHAPTER 6

IDENTIFY YOUR WANTS AND SET APPROPRIATE BOUNDARIES

One day Alice came to a fork in the road
and saw a Cheshire cat in a tree.
"Which road do I take?" she asked.
His response was a question: "Where do you want to go?"
"I don't know," Alice answered.
"Then," said the cat, "it doesn't matter."
Lewis Carroll, *Alice in Wonderland*
From Stephen Covey, *The 8th Habit*

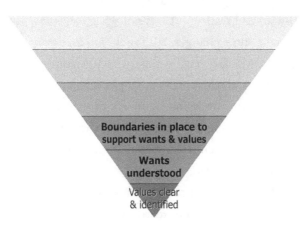

Boundaries in place to
support wants & values

Wants
understood

Values clear
& identified

Y ou are an executive, mother, and wife and have just been given a fantastic promotion. After much discussion with your three teenage kids and husband, you agree to accept it. Your family raised the concern that you will be working long days, and they will rarely see you. Not wanting to miss your family, you agree to be home for dinner at least three nights a week.

Over the next two to three months, your VP has asked you to stay late on numerous occasions because he said you write excellent reports. You were being asked to complete more and more reports that your department was responsible for. Although you haven't been home for dinner in several nights, you agree to work late again. You really love your work, you feel it is going well, and you think your family will understand.

That night you get home at 9 p.m., and your family is waiting up for you. They aren't happy and want a family meeting. Your husband and kids are frustrated because you aren't home like you said you would be, you are missing things with your kids, and they feel you care more about your work than you do about them. They need you and you aren't there.

Feeling awful and realizing this is not what you want, you recognize you need to make some changes. Although you love your work and the acknowledgment you are getting from the VP, your primary value is your family, and you don't want to disappoint them or let them down. You once again commit to being home for dinner at least three nights a week. This is something you recognize you want and supports your value of family. You are grateful to your family for their honesty and expression of their concerns.

The next day, the VP once again acknowledges your great work. Later in the afternoon, he comes to you with another report that needs to be completed for the next day, so he asks you to stay late to complete it. Thinking back to your family meeting, you are clear about what you want. You are committed to spending three nights with your family, so you politely decline the request of your VP, saying that you already have a commitment. While it was hard to say no to your VP, it felt good to say yes to your family.

What Do You Want?

So frequently when we ask clients, "What do you want?" they easily talk about what they don't want, but they can't clearly state what they do want. If we don't know what we want, how can we achieve it? Getting curious about what we want, and aligning our wants with our values, helps us focus on what we want to and can achieve.

When our client became clear about what she wanted and recognized that her wants aligned with her values, it became easier for her to say no to her VP so she could say yes to her family. In our hyper-connected, hyper-transparent world, the expectations of people are at an all-time high. It is impossible to be everything to everyone, so why try? Late meetings, additional assignments, bonus clients, networking dinners, extended deadlines, extra carpool, weekend birthday parties, class cupcakes, snack mom, room parent—the options are endless.

Identifying what you want allows you say yes to what you want and no to what you don't want.

Understanding what we want can be difficult, particularly when requests, invitations, and ideas are coming at us all the time. We invite you to reflect on your values and identify what you want that will support those values. Get curious about what each want looks like to you and how you can bring it into your life with clarity, so you can begin to embrace what you want and decline what you don't want. Sometimes you will still need to embrace something you may not want because it affects a greater want. For example, you may not want to be working a sixty-hour workweek right now, and a sixty-hour workweek may not be supporting your values. However, putting in a longer workweek now will support the possibility of achieving your greater want in the future (a promotion, putting new business systems in place, gaining new clients, etc.).

Use curiosity to explore your options, discover your wants, and gain clarity about how to incorporate your wants in your life so you can truly live your values. Like understanding your values, understanding your wants helps you become more self-aware, which will support you in your leadership, in building authentic relationships, and in emotional situations. (We will talk more about how our values are connected to our emotions in chapter 7).

Boundaries: Supporting What You Want

Boundaries are part of self-care.
They are healthy, normal, and necessary.
Dorren Virtue

Our personal boundaries are the non-negotiable rules or limits we set to identify what is permissible with ourselves and others. They define us as individuals in relation to others and protect us. Without boundaries, our lives feel chaotic and out of control. We take on everyone else's problems as our own, believe everyone else's bad behaviors are our fault, and feel like we are not entitled to any rights. None of us want to live like this!

To help you support your wants, you can set boundaries that help you say no with ease and grace. Boundaries can help you live your values so you can feel grounded, connected, and aligned with your inner truth. They allow your true self to emerge, so you can live in alignment with your wants and values. And they allow you to meet your needs first so you can better meet the needs of others.

Boundaries can also support you when you feel your emotional buttons being pushed, clarifying what is permissible and what is not, and how you want to move forward. They provide a framework in which to build your relationships. With boundaries, you get to choose how you want to build and support both your values and your wants, rather than passively accept what is brought to you.

Over the years, we have worked with a lot of different women from different backgrounds, experiences, ages, and ethnicities. One constant seems to be that they have few personal boundaries, which leads to emotional struggle, drama, and stress. Women struggle with putting up personal boundaries for a number of reasons: Some don't know what a boundary is, others don't realize they are allowed to have them, and still others don't understand how to use them. But most simply haven't identified what they want, so they don't know where to set a boundary in the first place.

Again, like your values and wants, your boundaries exist whether you identify them or not. Not understanding them and the need for them in relation to your wants and values can lead to your boundaries being too loose or too tight. Boundaries that are too tight can lead to feeling lonely, experiencing isolation, not letting anyone in, not asking for help, not talking about emotions or showing feelings, and having trust issues. Boundaries that are too loose can lead to feeling emotionally overwhelmed, experiencing lots of drama, giving too much, taking too much, feeling in constant need of reassurance, saying yes when you want to say no, feeling responsible for the feelings of others—lots of people pleasing.

Setting personal boundaries can be really hard. You may feel selfish, guilty, or embarrassed for honoring your wants first, which tends to be why so many women don't set them. However, not setting boundaries leads to feelings of resentment, anger, not being understood, constant complaining, and doing things you don't want to do. Like what you value and what you want in your life, your boundaries are personal, and they are there to support you in living in alignment with your true self.

Like so many others, I (Kirsten) have struggled with implementing boundaries. I talk with my friends and clients a lot about the lack of boundaries in our lives. We are trying to do it all, and often we are the ones who say yes when we should really be saying no.

When the kids were younger, I remember waking up to a text from a girlfriend who had offered to pick up my kids after school. She was going to take her kids with mine to the park to play and suggested I meet them later in the afternoon, giving me more time to work. I had picked up her kids a bunch of times and taken them to the park when she was busy, and now she wanted to return the favor.

With a pile of work that needed to be done, I got excited at this opportunity. I felt fortunate to have friends who looked out for me when they could and appreciated it. It felt like a win-win; my kids could play with their friends, which would make them happy, and I would get a couple of hours of extra work, which would make me happy—everyone's needs were met. I accepted, asked if she needed anything (she didn't), and with the new breathing room, I restructured my day to schedule an appointment with a client.

About thirty minutes before my kids were due to be picked up from school (five minutes before meeting a client!), I got a text from my girlfriend saying that she was too busy at work, had arranged a new playdate for her kids so she wouldn't have to leave work, and would not be able to pick up my kids as planned. She said it was better this way because she didn't have the car seats she needed for my kids, so I should be thankful she wasn't picking them up, and she hoped I would understand.

I remember reading it three times to be sure it said what it said. Understand? What part was I supposed to understand—that my family had been abandoned without a second thought to meet her needs, or that if we were not abandoned, my two young kids would have been riding around unsafely in her car?

Reeling from numerous emotions, I quickly snapped into action and cancelled my appointments with my client, which I hated to do. I was late picking up my kids from school, which my kids hated, their director hated, and I hated. I was angry for not honoring my client or my kids, hurt that my friend had no consideration for me or my family, and felt like every value was being stepped on along the way.

When I got home later that night and reflected on this situation, it became clear what I needed to do. The next morning I drew a lot of "lines," instilling very clear boundaries for myself. I was very clear with myself as to what was permissible and what wasn't. The needs of my family came first, and that included honoring our respect for time, safety, and commitments.

A few days later, this same friend called me close to pick-up time and wanted me to collect her kids from school. She was busy at work, and could I please just watch them? Pre-boundaries, I would have felt the need to say yes. I could sympathize with her situation and want to help friends when I can. That day I had promised my kids ice cream right after school, and while we could have delayed our arrival time, I had absolutely no problem respectfully saying no. I didn't give an excuse. I didn't even explain why. It was a clean and simple no. I chose to unapologetically honor the commitment to my kids, and it felt really good. As we all ate ice cream that afternoon, I silently vowed to instill more boundaries.

Group Boundaries

As managers, team leaders, leaders of organizations, or parents, it is important to identify group boundaries as well. When you identify the values and wants of an organization or family, boundaries can be put in place to support those values and wants, allowing the individuals within each to thrive. Clear expectations can help people align themselves with the values and wants of the organization/family. The boundaries not only support the organization/family, they support the individuals within them as well. The clearer we are with our organizational values, wants, and boundaries, the more likely we are to hire and attract those who are in alignment as well.

When to Set a Boundary

1. When you find yourself constantly complaining, feeling resentful, taken advantage of, angry, or compelled to do things you don't want to do
2. When you find yourself saying yes when you really want to be saying no

How to Set a Boundary

1. Get curious and explore where the feelings of frustration, anger, complaining, and/or resentment are coming from. What is happening for you to feel this way? What are you doing that you don't want to be doing? It is important to identify what

value is being compromised or the want you have that is not getting met.

2. Next, explore what you would like to see happen in your perfect world so you can get clear about what you want or what is permissible and what isn't. For example: If you get angry bringing home work every night and want to leave your work at the office so you can be home with your family, what boundary can you instill to support that want? In your perfect world, what would that look like? When is it permissible to bring work home, and when is it not permissible to bring work home?

3. If you find yourself saying yes when you want to be saying no, get curious about what is stopping you from saying no. How is this inability to say no supporting your values and your wants? What are you taking ownership of that is not yours to own? And what assumptions could you be making?

4. Once you have identified the reasons you feel you need to say yes, clarify what is permissible for you to say no to and what isn't. For example, Kirsten was clear about wanting to honor her commitment of taking her kids out for ice cream right after school, and it was important to her to keep it. While she wants to help friends when she can, helping her friend would have been at the expense of her kids and the promise she had made, which compromised both her values and her want. Setting a clear boundary of what was permissible and what wasn't (breaking a commitment and disappointing her kids) made it easy for her to draw a line and respectfully say no when she could have easily said yes.

5. As you set your boundaries, stay positive. With clear boundaries, you can believe in yourself and stay true to you.

6. Be assertive about your boundaries and respectful towards others in declaring them.

7. Show yourself some compassion. If others are offended when you say no to them, be kind to yourself.

8. Show others compassion as well. If you set clear boundaries around your wants and values, you can say no to others with respect, kindness, and generosity.

9. Use your boundaries to stay calm in emotional, messy situations with others. Being clear about your boundaries can help you remain separate from them.

Instilling boundaries is freeing and takes practice and consistency. The success of one boundary honored can fuel you to implement another. Now that we have explored how our boundaries support our wants, which in turn support our values and make it easier to live in alignment, let's look at how values, wants, and boundaries can help us better understand our emotions and emotional responses.

Take Action

Use the following chart to explore and clearly define what you want, clarify how your wants align with your values, and then set boundaries to help you achieve what you want. Think of clearly defining your wants as setting your destination for a journey and your values and boundaries as the GPS that will help keep you on your charted course to successfully arrive at that destination. Without setting a destination, you can't create a clear map to get there, and if you have no clear map, you will never arrive at your destination.

Top 3 Wants	What core values support your wants?	What boundaries can you set up to support your values and wants?
Example: Engage in respectful conversations	Respect	I ensure I am open and non-judging and I choose not to participate in gossip

CHAPTER 7

CONNECT YOUR VALUES
TO YOUR EMOTIONS

Control your emotion or it will control you.
Samurai maxim

Emotions connected to values

Boundaries in place to
support wants & values

Wants
understood

Values clear
& identified

107

J
ane is a leader who plays a demanding role in an organization where she is expected to be the troubleshooter. It is her job to deal with situations once they have gone wrong and have become a problem. Jane is also a client of ours.

One Friday she had a particularly difficult day where she was expected to resolve an issue arising out of the shipping department. A large order had been shipped to the wrong client, and the client who was supposed to have received the shipment needed it Saturday for an event. Given the size of the order, Jane's company did not have the quantity of product on hand needed by the client the next day.

Jane felt she had dealt with the situation but was still upset about it when she met her husband for dinner later at their favorite restaurant. She was late arriving, apologized, and then started to share the details of her difficult day. As she completed the first part of her story, sharing the problem, her husband jumped in and told her what to do to solve her problem, providing an overly simplified solution that did not take into account most of the variables that needed to be dealt with. Her husband also pointed out how he thought she could have addressed the situation in a much better way, implying she was wrong to have taken the approach she had.

Jane felt a surge of negative emotional energy flood her body. She lost it, telling him in no uncertain terms that he had no idea what he was talking about, that his solution was overly simplistic, and it would not address the problems at hand. Jane continued her rant, telling her husband she had figured out what to do. It was her problem, and she had dealt with it, finding a solution that ensured the product would be with the client by noon when it was needed. She *had* solved the problem!

And then she felt awful. She had said things to her husband that were inconsiderate, careless, and regrettable when her husband had just wanted to help, presenting a solution he thought might work.

How Our Values Connect to Our Emotions

On reflection, Jane identified one of her values to be accomplishment, and this value was nurtured when she was able to find solutions for problems that worked for everyone. This was true in any area of her life. When Jane heard her husband interrupt her and jump to a solution, she felt he was saying she couldn't solve the problem and achieve success on her own. Jane knew she could because she had. When she thought her husband was challenging her at the level of her deepest values, she immediately experienced negative emotions and reacted accordingly. Of course, Jane immediately regretted what she had said, and wished she could take back her words. But this was not an option.

We have all been here. I (Kathy) know I have. Someone says something that challenges my values, and I can feel negative emotions filling up my body. I become speechless and unable to think. I shut down and hate the feeling. I may not say anything; however, my non-verbal cues tell quite a story. I have been told my eyes tell the story and can stop a connection at twenty feet! If left long enough, I will continue to boil in silence until my nonverbal cues take over because, in some way, my body needs to express that I am not happy. I may slam a door, hiss a comment, or roll my eyes because I don't have the words to express what I am feeling. Fortunately for those around me, these outbursts are, for the most part, a distant memory. I have learned a different way to deal with such situations, and you can too.

So how did Jane deal with this? Jane decided she needed to get curious, explore what value had been tapped, and then acknowledge what happened so she could learn how to quiet these negative emotional surges. Jane wanted to remain calm and respectful in all conversations and ensure she did not say words she would later regret, words she could not take back.

One of the strategies Jane identified was to talk to her husband about what she needed. When she wanted to vent, she just wanted him to listen and support her without jumping to a solution. Jane shared this with him, and he agreed that in such situations, he would actively listen to understand her, perhaps be curious, and definitely support her. (These types of situations are also an opportunity for the listener to message support to the speaker through paraphrasing.)

What to Do with Negative Emotional Energy

Remember Kathy's neighbor who was still miffed at the end of the day because he had been kept waiting for forty-five minutes that morning? Or the owner of the sales company who was hurt and took over managing all the clients because she felt betrayed by her team? Or Kirsten's son who became an emotional wreck when he felt he wasn't being listened to and understood? When we are aware of and understand our values, we can begin to manage our response when we feel one of our values is disrespected.

Just as we need to take the time to identify our personal values and wants, we must also take the time to learn to manage our responses when they are tapped. The problem is that few of us have ever been taught to do this. When we take on a leadership role (personally or professionally) and have no skills or understanding regarding what to do when our emotional buttons are constantly getting pushed, we are setting ourselves up for failure. Most of us have been taught how not to react (don't yell, don't hit, don't be aggressive) or how to react appropriately (bite your tongue, smile, nod, hold back); however, how often do we take the time to get curious and examine why our emotions are triggered in the first place?

Yes, what's true about our values, wants, and boundaries is also true about our emotions: they are always present, whether we're conscious of them or not. When triggered, emotions can create feelings that tend to manage us rather than us managing them, which can be overwhelming. When those feelings are negative, allowing them to manage us can have devastating consequences. The good news is that clearly identifying your personal values is going to help you manage your emotional reactions in all areas of your life.

Once you are clear and comfortable with your own unique values, you can connect them to those surges of negative emotional energy and better understand what triggered this emotion. You can maintain your cool and feel in control, able to stay in the conversation without feeling like an uncontrollable force that rears its head as anger, shame, or blame. We know because we have learned to do this ourselves and have helped countless others find this place of calm, where you can stay rational, feel in control of your emotions, and seek to understand the perspectives of others. (In the next chapter, we'll show you how to find this place of calm, using the self-awareness you've been developing all along and specific calming strategies.)

You Have a Choice

Over the years, we have discovered that some people are not interested in learning to manage their emotions. They really like erupting, holding forth, and becoming accusatory towards others. They feel sometimes they just need to express themselves this way. On some level, it makes them feel good, full of energy. When asked how this supports their relationships, we have been told they often just don't care. The explosion is worth it.

Whatever your approach is, it is important to know that you always have a choice. You can decide when to erupt and when disrupting the relationship is not worth the rush. You can become the person focused on destroying everything in your path, *or* you can get curious, stay calm, and connect in conversation—the choice is yours. If erupting and disrupting consistently resonates with you, then we encourage you to get curious with yourself. What is motivating you to use this approach? What are you gaining, and what are you losing?

Emotions and Relationships

We have all been in a conversation where the other person seems to erupt in an emotional outburst out of the blue—shattering us and possibly the relationship. Connecting our values and emotions can help us stay connected in such situations.

It is the night before the much anticipated dance party, and Matt has been really looking forward to a night out dancing with his friends. Matt is soon to be a senior at school and is excited to be included in this party because many of the invited kids have already graduated. When he gets home, he tells his mom about the party.

As moms do, she starts asking some questions. Matt feels his mom is cool; she knows how badly he wants to go to this party and is honest in his answers. He can start to see his mom become hesitant in response to his answers. There are going to be some older kids at the party, and she doesn't love that. She says he can go, but they must agree that he can't stay out late.

Frustrated, Matt pleads with his mother, saying the party won't get started until late. He is going to be a senior next year—he wants to stay out late. He *needs* to stay out late. His mom says firmly, "No way. If you want to go, you must agree to be home by 11 p.m." Without missing a beat, Matt shouts, "You are not the boss of me!" and storms out, slamming the door behind him.

Matt is angry, frustrated, and hurt. He thinks to himself, "How could my mom do this to me? It is a dance party, everyone is going to be there, I am going to be a senior next year, and she is treating me like a baby. I was honest with her; I told her about the party before it happened, and now she is acting like she can't trust me!"

Meanwhile, Matt's mom Sara sits in the kitchen, going over in her head what just happened. Sara has two teenage kids and feels they have a close family unit. Her family is her number-one priority, what she values most. Sara wants Matt to go to the party; she knows it is important to him, but with the older kids invited, she is concerned about activities that might occur later on in the night, about which she thinks Matt has no experience. As his mother, it is her job to keep him safe. He doesn't know what these parties are like. She is hurt, thinking to herself, *How could he shout at me like that? I am his mother, and I am trying to protect him. Family is everything to me, and this is how he treats me.*

Sara feels truly "gutted" by this experience. She really believed she had a good relationship with her son, and after this, she begins to rethink this belief, because, in her eyes, her son didn't value their family. If he did, he would never have spoken to her like he did. She retreats, becoming very quiet, and he escapes, leaving the house and slamming the door behind him. Sara wonders how she is going to repair this situation and feel like her son is part of her close-knit family unit again.

Understanding Your Emotional Triggers

As mentioned above, Sara's number-one core value is family. She loves the warm feeling and sense of grounding and gratitude she experiences when others ask about her kids, their activities, her husband, or her parents, who have not been well. She feels her value of family is being respected. Think of a time when others have supported and acknowledged one of your core values. What was that like for you?

Now think of that same value and what happens when someone says or does something that ignores or disrespects it. How are you feeling now? With Sara, we saw how upset she was when Matt yelled at her: "You are not the boss of me!" She felt her value of family had been disrespected.

Matt similarly felt upset when his mom didn't respect his values. The difference was that Sara was aware of her value of family. While Matt knew that friends, independence, and trust were important to him, he didn't understand that his values connected directly to his emotions when not respected.

When we are able to understand that our values are connected to our emotions, it becomes easier to manage our emotions when our emotional buttons get pushed. Understanding our values allows us to put up boundaries to support ourselves in such situations, so we don't lose control and say or do things we later regret.

There Is No "I" in Us: Honoring Values in Others

While it is important to understand what our own personal values are to support how we manage our emotions, it is also important to recognize others have their own values, separate from us, that influence their emotions. Those values may not resonate with us or make sense to us, yet those values support emotions we need to be open to, curious about, and always respect.

Rarely will two people share the exact same values. And even if they do, the interpretation of those values will most likely not be the same. Expecting others to value what you do will only invite unwelcome emotional challenges for everyone.

Sara and Matt had their own sets of values they felt were disrespected and their own emotional buttons that got pushed, and both became upset, resulting in a fractured relationship. When we are not open to considering the values of others and focus solely on our own values, our values can act like blind spots, sabotaging relationships by focusing solely on our wants or needs without consideration for others.

Sara was still feeling emotional stress and tension when she contacted us the afternoon after her conversation with her son, Matt. She still hadn't seen Matt or talked to him. Sara had come to us initially to become curious as a leader. Through our work together, she learned the value of curiosity and its role in dealing with challenging conversations. Unsure of how she wanted to handle the situation with Matt, Sara began to explore different ways of being calm and found it helpful to visualize a place that relaxed her. It was grounding, calming, and necessary for her to access her self–awareness.

Sara wanted to understand what was going on for her. She needed to understand what was happening to her family. Sara knew she needed to speak to Matt. She decided she would need to access her place of calm and decide how to proceed with clarity before their conversation. (We are going to show you ways you can access your calming strategies in the next chapter.)

Before they met, using her calming strategies to access her self-awareness, Sara decided she wanted to be curious with her son in an effort to understand his reasons for feeling he needed to attend this party and stay late. She was curious to know his understanding of and experience with parties that involved mostly older kids. Sara knew she needed to test her assumptions about her ideas of such parties—she was making her experience as a teen his experience. Most importantly, she wanted to be curious about his comment to her: "You aren't the boss of me." Sara needed to understand what was behind his eruption and how they could work together to create a better way to have a conversation, as he continued to navigate the challenges of his teenage years.

When Matt came home later that afternoon, Sara invited him to sit with her so she could better understand what was going on for him. Although nervous and emotional, she calmly stayed curious by asking him curious open questions and listening to his responses with Choice 5 listening because she was very invested in the outcome of this conversation. Her desired outcome was to stay connected with her son. She intentionally kept the focus on him. Sara tested her assumptions, shared her concerns, and expressed empathy about the challenges of being a teenager. Digging deep within herself, she got curious about Matt's comment, how it impacted her value of family, and how it made her feel. She wanted to understand how they got to where they were, and how their relationship was going to move forward.

Here is what Sara learned: Her assumptions of parties with older kids were dead wrong. This party was a dance party where drugs and alcohol were prohibited. She learned her son had seen lots of kids out of control on drugs and/or alcohol, and the sense of no control held no interest for him. She learned Matt loved to dance. He just wanted to spend time dancing with his friends, which was fun for him. Sara learned of Matt's desire to be independent; he was trying to be more "adult" in how he lived his life. He felt that by coming to his mother a day before the party, he was showing maturity and responsibility. Her response frustrated him, as he felt she did not see him as being responsible, able to assess the inherent dangers that might be present at an event.

Sara learned a lot about her teenage son in ten short minutes and a lot about their relationship. Then something new happened— Matt thanked her for listening to him, sharing her perspective, and wanting to understand his. Family had been valued, their relationship authentically intact. It was seven quick words that put an angry ocean between them ("you are not the boss of me"). Sara could have grounded him, said no to the party, or gotten angry with him for how he spoke to her. But she didn't. Sara made a choice to respond differently—to respond curiously—and it resulted in new outcomes and opportunities for their relationship.

Just as we would like our values to be respected by others, it is important that we respect the values of others as well. It doesn't mean we have to share them or even like them; however, it does mean that we have to respect them. We can use curiosity to better understand others and their reasons for their values. We can identify boundaries that support our values so we don't feel vulnerable with others. Not only will curiosity result in a deeper understanding between you and others, it will help you avoid emotional conflict.

You now understand how your emotions are triggered when your values are not honored, respected, or acknowledged. You have also identified boundaries you can implement to support yourself. In the next chapter, we will be exploring calming strategies you can use to help you remain calm and access your Curiosity Skills when you feel your emotions triggered.

Take Action

Let's return to the chart you filled out in the previous chapter and fill in the gaps. For each of your top three wants, now fill in what happens when that value/want gets disrespected, and what emotional reactions occur for you.

If you find a particular comment or incident pushes your emotional buttons, but you can't connect it back to any defined core value or boundary, then explore further what the underlying value might be. Once you identify it, add it to your list and support it with a boundary. Further exploration may be needed to get each of your values named and defined in a way that truly works for you. (Remember, all of these charts can be downloaded for free at www.instituteofcuriosity.com.)

Understanding Your Emotional Triggers

Top 3 Wants	What core values support your wants?	What happens when that value/want gets disrespected or dishonored?	How do you react? What emotions come up for you?	What boundaries can you set up to support your values and emotions?
Example: Engage in respectful conversations	Respect	Lose respect for self and/or others	Get hurt, am disappointed, negative self-talk, feel defensive	I ensure I am open and non-judging and I choose not to participate in gossip

CHAPTER 8

ACCESS CALMING STRATEGIES

Calm can solve all issues.
Pole Shenouda

Calming strategies accessed

Emotions connected to values

Boundaries in place to
support wants & values

Wants
understood

Values clear
& identified

When we disagree with someone in conversation, or when someone disagrees with us, the emotional temperature of the conversation typically heats up, and before we know it, we find ourselves in conflict. Have you ever noticed that when someone becomes charged with negative emotional energy, you begin to feel it? Research shows the emotional energy between a speaker and listener is "contagious," so when someone in close proximity becomes volatile, the negative emotional energy that person is experiencing is transmitted to us, and we begin to feel the same way.[8] Now both people are filled with negatively charged emotional energy.

It is no secret that when our emotions boil we can't think straight, make smart choices, connect with others, have rational thoughts, and make realistic decisions. Our heart rate accelerates, our blood pressure increases, our muscles tense, and our stress levels surge. We operate from a place of fight-or-flight. It's not happy, and it can be unhealthy. We can learn how to manage our thoughts and feelings even when the negative emotional energy of another is transferred to us. We can move forward, using curiosity to help us see opportunities in such situations, rather than fixating on the problems that may have gotten us there in the first place.

We know that neuroscience findings indicate that curiosity produces dopamine and oxytocin, which both create a sense of feeling good. But how do you access curiosity when you feel overwhelmed, irrational, unable to think clearly, and eventually either become silent or erupt, saying things you would later regret? How do you access curiosity when you simply just don't care in that moment what the outcome is?

Self-Awareness: The Key to Managing Emotions

We define self-awareness as the understanding of one's values, wants, boundaries, and emotions. Having self-awareness puts us in the driver's seat when we feel we are spinning out of control due to our own negative emotional surge or that of someone close by. It allows us to see where our thoughts and feelings are taking us, both of which influence our behavior.

Based on our own experience and feedback from clients, we have learned that when we know what it feels like to be present in an unemotional "normal state" and what it feels like to be present when overcome by negative emotional energy, we will more easily notice the change as it happens. As we become aware of what our negative emotional energy feels like, we have the opportunity to bring our attention to it and consciously access our place of calm, get curious about what happened (i.e., what value was triggered), and use our Curiosity Skill of asking curious open questions.

We have found that after we ask our first curious open question, we notice a decrease in our negative emotional energy, and after the second curious open question, the negative emotional energy just washes away, replaced with a sense of feeling good. This practice has become easier over time, although we confess to the very occasional slip back into old patterns, typically with those we have been in a relationship with for a long, long time.

But even when we are completely self-aware and understand exactly what value or boundary has been crossed, we still may experience a negative emotional surge. We've found that regularly practicing calming strategies that put us in the habit of "being" rather than doing, and give us the regular opportunity to experience calm and tranquility, make it much easier to access a state of calm, and thus access our Curiosity Skills, when things heat up in the moment.

How to Be: Calming Strategies

Although there are several calming strategies one can practice, the idea is to find one (or maybe two) that really works and practice it on a regular basis so a sense of calm becomes natural and easy to access when confronted with a challenging situation. This sense of calm will allow you to "be" in the moment, gain focus, and remain curious. We have included seven strategies below that are popular with our clients and have helped them achieve calm so they can get curious.

Calming strategies are personal. What works for one may not work for another. If you find none of these strategies help you to feel calm and grounded, we encourage you to take the time to be curious and reflect. When do you feel calm? Where are you? What are you doing to access this feeling? Who are you with? What does it feel like? Practice accessing this "feeling" with no specific actions attached to it, so that in times of need you can take yourself there.

1. Meditation

Meditation is an ancient practice that has been used to quiet the mind and calm people for centuries. Originating in India, meditation became somewhat popular in North America in the 1960s and has been embraced by thousands of people since then. Many different types of meditation can be explored, and some are said to have specific medicinal benefits.

Benefits: Although the practice of meditation has been around for centuries, it is receiving a fair amount of attention these days as more and more researchers are recognizing its health benefits.[9] The practice of meditation is a process of connecting with who you are intrinsically. Through meditation, you become less re-active and more responsive. Meditation supports the understanding that life, for you, is about how you see it, your perspective. It supports an understanding that you are not your thoughts. You witness your thoughts, but they don't define you, which can be incredibly useful and powerful in moments of emotional distress, giving you space to use curiosity to understand. Benefits of meditation include: increased focus, improved memory, increased self-peace, improved self-acceptance, improved self-confidence, sleeping and waking more easily, improved relationships, and less drama/conflict.[10]

Meditation offers the space to reflect, learn, and get curious, allowing you to discover opportunities you would not normally consider. "Being" instead of "doing" for even a brief time will provide the grounding and sense of calm that will help you gain clarity about what you want to do.

Challenges: Meditation can feel hard to do, especially if you don't like to sit still. Many picture "meditation" as sitting cross-legged and still for hours at a time. Did you know that there are hundreds of different types of meditation? Walking, cooking, and bike riding can all be forms of meditation. It isn't the way you meditate that's important, but the stillness of mind you access. Curious to try it and don't know how to start? Visit www.instituteofcuriosity.com for a free ten-minute guided daily meditation.

2. Deep Breathing

This practice has also been around for centuries and is used to help find a place of calm and tranquility. As the name implies, this involves intentional deep breaths in and out, while one focuses on his or her breathing.

Benefits: This is a popular choice with clients, as anyone can achieve a sense of calm by taking a few deep breaths. Deep breaths are also easy to do in the moment and can be done without others even noticing. Benefits of deep breathing include releasing tension, gaining clarity, releasing toxins, releasing emotional stress, improving posture, boosting energy, and elevating mood. Athletes can often be seen at a starting line taking a few deep breaths as part of their preparation for a race. This helps them stay calm so they can focus on what lies ahead and their strategy for winning while staying connected to their hearts. Our experience has shown that it is good to practice this strategy when a negative emotional surge is absent, so it is familiar and easy to access when you feel challenged and need to access it.

Challenges: We aren't familiar with any.

3. Visualization

A form of meditation, visualization is the process of creating a mental picture of something that we want to manifest in our reality. People love to picture themselves in a favorite location (at the beach, in nature, or in the mountains), complete with details that can involve all the senses. Some also enjoy picturing themselves calm and relaxed.

Benefits: When practiced on a regular basis, people claim they can quickly access their visualization and move there easily in a way that provides them with a sense of calm and even lead to a sense of joy. Benefits of visualization are: increased focus, increased relaxation, decreased blood pressure, increased clarity, increased creative inspiration, increased self-confidence, increased sense of calm, and increased mind/heart connection.

Challenges: When people use this strategy to prepare for a conversation, an interview, or a meeting, they may find this strategy challenging if they have "visualized" a conversation or a scenario, and it doesn't go the way they planned or visualized. They end up experiencing more stress because it didn't go the way they wanted. When using this strategy, it is important to approach it from a place of openness. The intention of this strategy is to bring yourself to a place of tranquility and reconnect to yourself, so that you gain control over your emotions and can access your Curiosity Skills. If you choose to visualize a meeting or a conversation, visualize to clearly define the outcome you want, not the specific details of how you will get there. Then, enter such a meeting/conversation grounded, focused on the desired outcome, and completely open, ready to use your Curiosity

Skills. Being grounded, focused, open, and curious will help you in achieving the outcome you desire.

4. Seeking Solitude

Life can be hectic and overwhelming. Whether you find yourself moving from one meeting to another very quickly or just trying to complete the expectations and demands of your day, seeking solitude is an easy way to feel a sense of calm in a hectic schedule. One strategy clients have told us about is a bathroom break. Toilet stalls are private and can provide the solitude needed to access a place of calm. Some find a little hideaway within a building where they can go for just a couple of minutes, and others take time for a cup of tea and give themselves permission to just "be," allowing themselves to get grounded and feel calm.

Benefits: Seeking solitude allows you to reboot and unwind, increases concentration, and improves productivity, giving you pause to reflect and find your voice.

Challenges: We aren't familiar with any.

5. Humming

Humming is considered to be a soothing form of sound medicine. Filling your head with the vibrations of a calming hum can offer instant calmness and a sense of bliss. Many claim it helps them regain a sense of composure so they can access their curiosity and move forward.

Benefits: Humming helps ground and connect you to your center, promotes clarity of thinking, has a relaxing effect on face and neck, releases stress, slows down breathing and calms the nervous system, lowers blood pressure, and puts a smile on your face.[11]

Challenges: Humming around others can be distracting, intimidating, or render you self-conscious, which is not helpful when wanting to use a calming strategy. If you are interested in this strategy, we suggest you combine it with seeking solitude and find a quiet place where you can be alone and hum.

6. Positive Self-Talk

Is your glass half empty or half full? Some people can successfully be their own cheerleader and carry out a pep rally for one. If this sounds like you, positive self-talk can help you access a sense of being, a place of calm and optimism, where you can connect to your deepest self and even reframe beliefs as new possibilities. Staying positive with yourself and your outlook on life allows you to live a happy, fulfilling, and healthy life. Remember: thoughts create actions, which produce results.

Benefits: Engaging in positive self-talk can boost your confidence, calm your emotions, and create new thoughts, which support different actions and produces powerful new results. Positive self-talk increases confidence, keeps one's mind open to new possibilities, supports a positive attitude (which leads to seeing good in people and situations), increases optimism, increases opportunity, and increases self-acceptance.

Challenges: This practice can be challenging if you are prone to negative self-talk. Negative self-talk will influence your thoughts, which creates actions that don't produce new or different results. Negative self-talk can be destructive and judgmental, sabotaging health and happiness. There are no benefits to negative self-talk. If you find yourself unable to let go of negative self-talk, then we encourage you to get curious about understanding where it is coming from and your reasons for holding onto it. We also encourage you to try another calming strategy.

7. Time Out

If you don't regularly practice other calming strategies and need an immediate way to defuse your negative emotions in the moment, we've found that the best solution is to give yourself permission to take a time out to cool off and reflect. When you feel pressured, unprepared, overwhelmed, highly emotionally charged, and/or out of control, taking a time out may be necessary and beneficial. Asking for a minute to yourself can help you collect yourself or put up a boundary if you feel your space is being invaded. This strategy is sometimes used in negotiations and provides the parties with the space to rethink what they really want.

Benefits: Taking a time out creates the space for you to reflect. It allows you to regroup, cool off, ground yourself, consider your perspective, get clear on what you want, and support your boundaries.

Challenges: For some, a time out communicates weakness. They feel having to leave a situation, even for a few minutes, indicates a lack of skill or an inability to stay in the challenging conversation and (perhaps) shout your way out of it. If a time out is a calming and an empowering strategy for you, then we encourage you to focus on your needs and embrace a time out, so you provide a positive message to those around you. If you are on the fence and feel it could be seen as a weakness, then we encourage you to avoid this strategy, as that is what you will communicate. The idea is to find a strategy that supports you in finding your center, your sense of self and calm, so that you can access curiosity.

When practiced regularly, strategies such as these are going to help you access your inner calm, develop your self-awareness, and understand/control your emotional triggers—all helping you access curiosity to understand how you want to proceed. Investing in your self-awareness will support your leadership, your relationships, and your overall health and happiness.

In Parts One and Two, you've learned the three Curiosity Skills and how to apply those skills in order to understand yourself. In Part Three, we're going to bring it all together and show you how to apply the Power of Curiosity method to our most difficult interactions with others.

Take Action

We invite you to try a few calming strategies, and find at least one that works for you. Practice it often so you can easily access it when and if you need it. Be curious in your practice, and see what comes up for you, how you feel, and how your strategy supports you in your daily life.

Part Three

USING CURIOSITY TO UNDERSTAND OTHERS

CHAPTER 9

THE MILLION-DOLLAR ANSWER

Peace is not absence of conflict;
it is the ability to handle conflict by peaceful means.
Ronald Reagan

Open to exploring new opportunities
and outcomes using Curiosity Skills

Calming strategies accessed

Emotions connected to values

Boundaries in place to
support wants & values

Wants
understood

Values clear
& identified

A t the beginning of our workshops, we like to check in with the participants and see what their goals are for the time we spend together. Although we have a specific agenda, we are curious about the needs of those who are joining us. How can we meet the needs of our clients if we don't understand what they truly want? So we always ask, "What is the one thing you want to walk away with today that would make your time with us successful?" Every time it is the same answer: "I want strategies to use when I disagree with someone and find myself in conflict with them. How can I have drama-free conversations?"

Therein lies the million-dollar question. How do we have an authentic exchange of thoughts and feelings, one that promotes respectful, productive dialogue and leads us to a place of calmness, confidence, and abundance—even in high-stakes situations?

The million-dollar answer is the Power of Curiosity method you have been learning throughout this book. Without the Curiosity Skills, even the most respectful conversations can become telling, blaming, and shaming—which leads to conflict. Curiosity allows you to have respectful conversations that don't lead to conflict: necessary conversations that have been too easy to ignore (addressing the elephant in the room); productive conversations that can become stressful and emotional in the moment; and challenging conversations where you are invested in the outcome.

Respectful Conversations

We all have the ability to have respectful conversations all the time, conversations in which we understand the needs and perspectives of all involved. However, even the most respectful conversations can become hair raising or confrontational when curiosity is absent. You can achieve respectful conversations consistently when you use your Curiosity Skills to better understand the speaker(s). When we have a strong understanding of self (our values, wants, boundaries, and emotional triggers), it becomes easier to focus on the speaker and be curious about them. Our understanding shifts us away from needing to tell, judge, blame, and shame. When we become curious about others, we deepen our understanding of who they are, which creates stronger connections and richer relationships. It also creates opportunities and possibilities that would not normally exist. Our success and happiness in life are directly correlated to the relationships we build, and we always have a choice in how we build them.

The Elephant in the Room

Years ago, when I (Kathy) was working as an occupational therapist, I worked at large organizations, developing strategies to support those struggling at work either to stay at work or return to work with modifications so they could transition back to full-time employment. I cannot tell you how many times I met with employees who were struggling, or off work, because they felt anxious and pressured to do more work than they had ever done before. They did not understand why their managers were being "heavy handed" with them, creating expectations they considered to be unrealistic.

When I talked to the managers, typically new in the role, it was commonplace for me to be told the employees had been getting away with inappropriate behavior and low productivity for up to twenty-five years. These new managers were finally going to deal with the situation, one that had been allowed to fester for way too long. Although the action was most likely an appropriate one, you can imagine how the employees felt, having their productivity challenged after so many years of no feedback about any aspect of their performances.

For years, most managers did not have the skills to deal with poor performance and chose to ignore the behavior rather than talk about it and support employees in making changes so their performance met expectations. They knew such conversations would be challenging and confrontational, and things might be said that could be regretted later. It was easier to avoid such situations, ignore behavior, and allow things to remain status quo. This approach is bad for the employer (via poor productivity), impacts everyone else in the department as they watch one employee slack off while they work hard, and reflects badly on the employees and their managers.

This approach can no longer continue. We need to address the elephant in the room when it shows up, not twenty-five years later! Managers need to address performance issues in a supportive way, where they use Choice 5 listening, are curious about the perspectives of the employee, and focus the employee on making the necessary changes to enhance productivity.

How often have you witnessed this in a work environment? You notice employees "getting away with murder" while the manager chooses to avoid the necessary discussions, and the inappropriate or counterproductive behaviors continue. What message does this send to you? How much respect do you have for this manager? If this goes on for an extended period of time, how does it impact the culture of the workplace?

Such experiences are not restricted to the workplace. They are common at home as well—family "situations" that are ignored or swept under the rug until an event such as a family wedding, a Thanksgiving dinner, or a family funeral, where everyone is expected to attend. Not attending may not be an option due to pressure from family members who want everyone to share in their joy or provide support in their grief. Many families have "skeletons in the closet" that cause challenges when any family gathering is scheduled. Some families expect everyone to get along at any cost; conversation becomes superficial, and time spent together is minimized to meet the wishes of everyone. Such "elephants" can linger in these situations for years, or they can be addressed in a way that ensures everyone involved feels seen, heard, and understood.

Productive Conversations When
Negative Emotions Are Present

Based on our experience, we believe the reason people say they want to avoid conflict is because they don't feel comfortable having conversations when conflict is present. When someone openly disagrees with their perspective and they sense a rise in negative emotional energy, many people begin to have a sense of feeling blindsided and out of control, and they don't know why. Words become hostile, negative emotional energy rises, and everyone involved reverts to Choice 2 or 3 listening, filled with telling and judging. Rarely do such conversations have productive outcomes. Words are said that are later regretted, or one retreats into silence. Relationships break down, trust can be lost, and it isn't good for our health.

But as we now know, conflict doesn't begin with the negative emotional outburst, it begins at the level of our values.

When we are vague and unclear about our values, wants, and boundaries, it is much more difficult for us to be self-aware when our emotional buttons get pushed, making it impossible to think clearly, calmly, or curiously in order to understand what we want and how to move forward. Staying in this place of discomfort results in avoidance, assumptions, judging, blaming, and shaming. Old patterns continue and relationships fracture, drastically limiting possibilities and outcomes.

Every time you enter into a conversation, you always have choices. You choose how you are going to listen, you choose how deeply you want to understand, and when the going gets tough, you choose whether you want to erupt/retreat into silence *or* find a place of calm and curiosity to discover new possibilities. Curiosity is your most powerful tool—a tool you can use in any conversation to better understand what has been said, why it has been said, what is going on for the other person, and what is going on for yourself. Curiosity is the key to resolving conflict so that relationships remain intact, and the challenges are respectfully resolved.

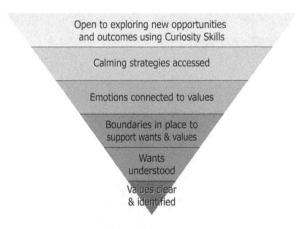

As we've learned throughout this book, being tight and clear on your values, wants, and boundaries allows you to be open and curious in conflict, accessing calming strategies to keep uncomfortable conversations drama and stress free. We have also found that when we intentionally use our Curiosity Skills in challenging conversations—when we become present to ABSORB, choose how we want to listen, and ask just one curious open question—negative emotional energy begins to dissolve.

As we continue to actively listen and then ask a second curious open question, the grip of emotion that takes hold gradually loosens. As we continue in this way, we start to feel good, and the negative wash of emotion becomes a distant memory. As the negative emotional energy dissipates from us, then the other person begins to experience the same fading of the emotional surge. Options for moving forward are limitless, full of possibility.

Looking at the two diagrams, which one are you currently using in such conversations?

When emotions run high, we know it takes work to remain calm and curious. Our default is to become defensive, judgmental, blaming, and shaming (internally and/or externally) without ever intending to do so. It just happens. We also know the key to challenging conversations and dealing with conflict is curiosity. It helps you stay calm, clear, understanding, and be open to new opportunities.

Challenging Conversations with a Desired Outcome

Imagine you are a nurse. You work with a physician who makes you feel intimidated. After your interactions with her, you always leave feeling like you have done something wrong, even when you know you have no reason to feel this way. Earlier in the week, this physician's actions upset one of your patients. You specifically requested that the physician approach this patient in a certain way, as the patient was very sensitive, and the physician disregarded your request. Your patient is now really upset and in need of an apology. You knew the physician could be insensitive when she was in a hurry, and you appreciate the pressures of her job. You also understood the fragile state of your patient, which is why you specifically requested the patient be approached in a certain way.

Part of your job is to ensure patients are taken care of and have a good experience while getting the necessary care. After the way this physician treated your patient, you know you need to have a talk with her. You are nervous, intimidated, and frustrated that you were ignored. You value your professionalism and feel disrespected. You feel you haven't done anything wrong, don't appreciate being disregarded, and don't want to be blamed for something you didn't do. You wish the physician had just listened to you, so you wouldn't be in this position to begin with.

You may often find yourself in a situation where you know a conversation with someone could get messy. Entering into such a conversation blind, with no desired outcome, can make it more challenging to keep your cool and not make a messy situation messier. Understanding what you want before you enter such a conversation will help you remain open, using Curiosity Skills to keep the focus on the outcome. We have learned this because we have spent a great deal of time supporting and coaching others using this strategy.

When I (Kathy) met with this frustrated client, the nurse, she decided to take some time to get curious about what she wanted from her conversation with this physician before she met with her. After some preparation, she asked to meet with the physician and agreed to do it in the physician's office. This client approached the physician with her goal in mind: a patient who felt respected. After providing context for the meeting, this client chose to become curious with the physician, asking her the reasons she said what she did to the patient. She pointed out notes written on the file advising her to be cautious in her choice of words due to the patient's fragile state.

At first, the physician became defensive. While not the way our client was hoping the conversation would go, she chose to stay curious, holding her end goal in mind: a patient who felt respected. After asking a second curious open question, the physician began to relax. She could see the nurse was listening to her (using Choices 4 and 5) and asking open questions that were not judging. It became clear the nurse wasn't here to blame her; the nurse was here to understand. The conversation moved forward with this client continuing to ask curious open questions and choosing to actively listen to understand, not judge or blame. The emotion of the conversation was neutralized. The physician indicated she had not had time to read the notes the nurse had written because she was behind schedule and didn't feel the notes would be helpful while she was completing the procedure with the patient. As each of them began to understand the other and the situation with their patient, our client shared afterwards, she could feel their relationship changing and becoming more equal and respectful.

At the end of the conversation, the physician agreed to drop by their patient's room and apologize to him. The nurse felt she had achieved her goal. She said she stayed curious and open at all times and kept her goal in mind as she conversed with the physician. She felt really good about the conversation when it was completed and recognized the potential Curiosity Skills provided in such situations.

As you just experienced with our client, preparing for such a conversation by defining your goal, your outcome, and what success will look like help you to stay focused on your goal. When you combine that process with curiosity, you can navigate whatever comes your way, staying calm, curious, and open to the perspective of the other person or persons. So frequently we approach such a conversation, thinking, '"We need to make our point," "We need to show them we are right," or "We need to show them they are wrong." Having such a mindset when one approaches a conversation can have a similar effect to a belief, blindsiding us so we shut out other perspectives, and we use Choices 1, 2, or 3. We are judging what is being said, if we are listening at all. How helpful is this?

We have found when people take the time to identify their desired outcome of the conversation (for our client, the outcome was patients feeling respected), are present to actively listen, use Choice 4 listening to understand the speaker, and ask curious open questions to support their desired outcome (supported by Choice 5 listening), the emotion of the conversation dissipates and shifts away from judging, blaming, and shaming to understanding and learning—a win-win for all.

Strategy for Conversations Where You Have a Desired Outcome

1. Define your goal: What do you want to achieve in this conversation that is not judging, blaming, or shaming?
2. Determine where you want to meet and for how long.
3. Identify what you need to do to stay calm and aware during the conversation.
4. Use your Curiosity Skills:
   a. Be present and ABSORB to actively listen,
   b. Listen using Choices 4 and 5,
   c. Ask curious open questions.
5. Test assumptions or beliefs.
6. Reframe for new possibilities.
7. Continue to use your Curiosity Skills to stay curious and focused on your goal.
8. Conclude the conversation.

Take Action

You are clear on your values, wants, and boundaries; you understand your emotional triggers; and you can access your calming strategies. When you feel the heat rise in a conversation or you're tempted to retreat, access your million-dollar tool: the Power of Curiosity method.

1. Use your Curiosity Skills (Be Present to ABSORB, Use Listening Choices 4 and 5, and Ask Curious Open Questions) to support yourself in the moment to better understand the other person.

2. Whenever you feel your emotions rise, access your calming strategies and ask a curious open question, which will also help neutralize the emotions of the speaker.

3. If you find yourself in Choice 1, 2, or 3 listening, use curious open questions to get you back to Choice 4 and 5 to better understand the speaker.

4. If you have identified an outcome for the conversation, stay present and focus on the outcome using the ABSORB process, Choice 4 listening to understand the speaker, and curious open questions with Choice 5 listening to facilitate the desired outcome and establish accountability for all involved.

5. Whenever you find the conversation descending into a place of judging, telling, blaming, or shaming, use your Curiosity Skills to better understand what is going on for the speaker (and yourself).

6. If at any time you feel overwhelmed, respectfully ask for a moment to walk away or pause, collect yourself, access your calming strategy, and ask yourself, "What am I curious about? What do I want out of this? How can I look at this differently?"

Your goal is to consistently remain curious with yourself and others. Curiosity will support the understanding needed to resolve the conflict/ challenge, as well as create new opportunities and possibilities that would not otherwise be available to you.

YOUR NEXT STEPS

Change is hard. Our very human nature pulls us back to the status quo,
not because it is better, but because it's familiar.
Brigid Schulte, *Overwhelmed*

Y ou now hold the power of curiosity in your hand, and your next
steps are up to you. You can choose to shelve this book with
all your other self-help books and simply hope things will be
different, or you can choose to take what is in your hand and apply
it to achieve true understanding and the transformative outcomes
you want. The choice is yours. Either way, we ask that you think of
our time together as an investment in yourself, your future, your
family, and your career. So as you think of your next steps, we ask,
what would be the cost to incorporate curiosity into your life (your

leadership, your family, your relationships)? What would be the cost if you didn't?

We aren't here to make promises we can't keep or overwhelm you with redundant information. It was our goal to open your eyes to new possibilities, gaining a deeper understanding of yourself and others through the power of curiosity.

You now know your values and your wants and have created some boundaries that will help you live the life you want, free of the beliefs that no longer serve you. Building on this, you have developed a greater sense of self-awareness by understanding your emotional triggers and identifying calming strategies you can access when you feel the beginning of a negative emotional surge. All of these will help you access your Curiosity Skills when conflict arises, allowing you to have the conversations you want.

Once curious, you can recognize which value has been tapped and then become curious about the other person. You can paraphrase to gain clarity and communicate that you are present and actively listening. Perhaps you can test an assumption, challenge a belief, or reframe it.

Knowing you are about to have a conversation that could be challenging and confrontational, you can plan for it, defining your desired outcome so you can stay the course and hold on to that outcome as you use your Curiosity Skills to better understand others. As you actively listen to them from a place of calm, they will also become calm and better understand your perspective. As you continue to better understand each other, you can appreciate each other's perspective. You may choose to disagree with the other person, *and* you still understand and appreciate their thoughts, their ideas, and their values. The relationship remains intact, and the connection is enhanced. You can now continuously engage in respectful conversations and transform conflict from a negative experience into a positive opportunity.

As you move forward, we ask you to embrace these three things to support your success:

1. Practice your Curiosity Skills! Don't save these skills for a special occasion; use them daily and use them freely. The more you practice, the easier it will become. Don't expect to have perfected each skill just by reading this book. What you put into your life is what you will get out of it, and these three Curiosity Skills are no different. Take the time to identify your values, wants, and boundaries, and use your Curiosity Skills to support yourself. If you want to achieve truly transformational results, then practice and participate in all the components of our method. We assure you, with consistent practice and intention, you will find that it becomes hard *not* to be curious.

2. Have patience with yourself. Doing new things and trying different approaches takes time and patience. Sometimes the outcome may not be what you expected, but any outcome will provide new learning as long as you remain curious. For many people, it will require unlearning what has taken them a lifetime to perfect, so don't expect for this new journey to be quick and easy. If you find yourself slipping into old patterns that don't support curiosity or understanding, stop and ask a curious open question: "What am I curious about?" "How can I look at this differently?" "What can I learn?" Be kind with yourself as you embark on your new learning journey, and be kind to others who are on their own learning journey—it may not be like yours. Regardless of where you find yourself, have patience and always be curious.

3. Give yourself permission to do it differently. Letting go of a belief or an assumption that you have carried around for years and doesn't serve you can be tough. Setting a boundary that you have never set before (and sticking to it!) can feel scary and challenging. Honoring your values and wants may come at the expense of others, which is never easy. Give yourself permission to move forward differently, which may mean letting go of the way you used to do things or *should* be

doing things. Let go of telling, fixing, judging, and blaming (of self and others) and embrace learning and understanding through curiosity. Take risks, ask questions, and commit to achieving the new outcomes and transformations you desire. We all have a story, and the only person who can change yours is you.

Wanting to ensure your success, we have created a workbook that is available at www.instituteofcuriosity.com. This workbook will help you take your learning journey to the next level of success. In it, you will find all the Take Action exercises and charts from this book, as well as additional exercises, reflections, and challenges that will help you further develop your three Curiosity Skills, your understanding of yourself, and your understanding of others. Discover how present you truly are, outline a map to achieve what you want, and discover more tools for challenging conversations.

As a mother/daughter team, we have learned that if we don't change how we do what we do, nothing ever changes—there are never new opportunities, possibilities, results, or changed outcomes. Without curiosity, relationships fracture, and understanding and connection are lost. We live in a time where change is constant, and our future depends on new possibilities and innovative outcomes. We know the old way no longer works, so let's begin a new way, together. We all have the ability to achieve greatness and understanding in everything we do. We invite you to choose to live a life absent of judging, blaming, and shaming, one that is filled with respect, understanding, and curiosity. Respectful understanding is a choice, and you now have the method to achieve it. That is the Power of Curiosity.

WITH GRATITUDE

This book is the culmination of ten years of learning, and we believe learning is what life is all about. The stories we describe in this book are based on conversations and feedback shared with us by our clients, those whom have inspired us so much. To protect confidentiality, the stories are an amalgamation of the learning moments they shared with us. We are deeply grateful for our opportunity to partner with so many enthusiastic, open, and curious leaders, and you all know who you are. Thank you all so very much, particularly those many leaders at the Provincial Health Services Authority in British Columbia, where this learning journey started and evolved through curiosity.

We extend a very special thank you to Amanda Rooker, our editor, whose support and commitment to this project has been so appreciated. Although we found it challenging at times to write with clarity, Amanda provided the focus and asked the questions that helped us be clear and organized in the presentation of our thoughts and elegant with our ideas.

This journey began with Dori Van Stolk, Director of Learning at BC Children's Hospital, who saw the value of curiosity in supporting learning, particularly for midlevel leaders. Her foresight provided an opportunity for us to collaborate and build a program that used curiosity to develop leadership focused on understanding the perspectives and needs of others. We are immensely grateful to Dori for her support.

Others who began this journey with us include Erna Hagge, who co-created and co-presented the workshops for the leadership program, and Deb McDougall, Riola Crawford, and Teresa Belluz, all of whom supported the work we were doing and integrated it into their training workshops in leadership development. Support for us as newbie authors came from Alexandra Leh, who helped us find our voices as would-be writers, and Johanie Marcoux, whose help once the book was completed has been so appreciated.

And lastly, we are grateful to our colleagues, friends, and family, who have provided us with so much support along the way. Your continued belief in us has been greatly appreciated, and without it, we probably would have stumbled one too many times. Believing in our ability to write this book *and* work together as a mother/daughter team has helped us to continue to believe in ourselves. Thank you!

Most important is our gratitude for each other, having the opportunity to work together and partner in creating this book has been a gift both of us truly appreciate. I (Kathy) am so grateful to have the continued opportunity to partner with my daughter on this learning journey, to work with her on a daily basis even with 3,000 miles between us. We have learned to be curious with each other, to learn from each other, and to truly understand each other. I think we had a good mother/daughter relationship as we both "grew up," and now that relationship has become so much more. Thank you, Kirsten, for believing in me, partnering with me to better understand the power of curiosity, and sharing our knowledge with the world. I think we both believe that, collectively, we can change the world, one conversation at a time.

All of the good parts of this book we attribute to the learning created as we all worked together, while the errors and omissions are solely our responsibility.

Kathy and Kirsten

ABOUT THE AUTHORS

A former occupational therapist with a master's degree in leadership and a Professional Certified Coach through the International Coach Federation, Kathy Taberner has been a facilitator/trainer and coach in leadership development for the past ten years. After recognizing how crucial curiosity was to understanding others and building relationships, she and her daughter, Kirsten Taberner Siggins, co-founded the Institute of Curiosity, a coaching and training organization that helps individuals learn and apply the skills of curiosity to their personal and professional relationships. Kathy lives in the Okanagan Valley and Vancouver with her husband.

Kirsten Taberner Siggins is a certified executive coach and a member of the International Coaching Federation, with experience in the business world and the entertainment industry (Warner Music London,

American Idol, and AOL RED, as well as producing events, photo shoots, and commercials). Regardless of industry or context, Kirsten believes curiosity is essential to personal success, growth, innovation, health, and happiness, and co-founded the Institute of Curiosity with her mother, Kathy Taberner, in 2014. Kirsten lives in Los Angeles with her husband and two children.

NOTES

1   Zosia Bielski, "Overwhelmed: Why We Need to Take Back Leisure Time," *The Globe and Mail* online, April 1, 2014, http://www. theglobeandmail.com/life/relationships/too-busy-to-live-in-a-contemporary-world/article17758066/.

2   August Turak, "Steve Jobs and the One Trait All Innovative Leaders Share," *Forbes* online, November 21, 2011, http://www. forbes.com/sites/augustturak/2011/11/21/steve-jobs-and-the-one-trait-all-innovative-leaders-share/.

3   Judith E. Glaser, *Conversational Intelligence* (Bibliomotion, 2014), 131.

4   Alan B. Krueger, "Superiority of Group Decision Making: 'Economic Scene,'" *The New York Times,* December 7, 2000, C2, quoted in Daniel Goleman, Richard Boyatzis, and Annie McKee, *Primal Leadership* (Harvard Business School Press, 2002), 173.

5 "Mehrabian's Communication Study," *ChangingMinds.org*, June 4, 2012, www.changingminds.org/explanations/behaviors/body_language/mehrabian.htm.

6 Gervase Bushe, *Clear Leadership* (Davies-Black Publishing, 2001).

7 Stephen R. Covey, *The 8th Habit: From Effectiveness to Greatness* (Free Press, 2004).

8 Roland Neumann and Fritz Strack, "'Mood Contagion': The Automatic Transfer of Mood between Persons," *Journal of Personality and Social Psychology* 79, no. 2 (August 2000), 211–222.

9 "Does Meditation Have Benefits for Mind and Body?" *Medical News Today*, February 26, 2014, http://www.medicalnewstoday.com/articles/272833.php.

10 Deedee Poyner, energy healer and meditation instructor, www.deedeepoyner.com.

11 Carole Fogarty, "The 12 Instant Benefits of Humming Daily," *The Healthy Living Lounge*, http://thehealthylivinglounge.com/2009/08/06/12-instant-benefits-of-humming-daily/, accessed August 7, 2014.

Printed in the USA
CPSIA information can be obtained
at www.ICGtesting.com
JSHW082337140824
68134JS00020B/1727

9 781630 473945